ONE FOR
THE ROAD

MISADVENTURES

Sydney- Paris Link

Other works by Alister Kershaw written in Paris

Accent & Hazard (Paris 1951)

Murder in France (London 1955)

A History of the Guillotine (London 1958)

A Word from Paris (Sydney 1991)

Works by Alister Kershaw written in France

Heydays (1991)

Collected Poems (1993)

The Complete Poems of Mort Brandish (1994)

A Second Denuciad (1994)

One for the Road (2003)

ONE FOR THE ROAD

MISADVENTURES

—

ALISTER KERSHAW

ETT IMPRINT

Exile Bay

This edition published by ETT Imprint, Exile Bay 2022

A later version of this book was first published by Terry Risk at the Typographeum, Francetown, New Hampshire in 2003.

First electronic edition published by ETT Imprint 2022

ETT IPRINT
PO Box R1906
Royal Exchange NSW 1225
Australia

ISBN 978-1-922698-13-1 (paper)
ISBN 978-1-922698-14-8 (ebook)

Cover and illustrations by Robin Wallace Crabbe
Design and frontespiece by Tom Thompson

A Sydney-Paris Link publication
in memory of Jean-Paul Delamotte

For Sylvain & Solange

ONE

None of the neighbours made a sign to ward off the evil eye when we passed each on the on the road. I could hardly believe my luck. It was practically tantamount to being welcomed with open arms. Thirty-five years ago when I settled in the French countryside the old peasant traditions were pretty much as they had been for centuries past. Wariness where strangers were concerned was one of those traditions. My closest neighbour, Maxime, was even warier than the others. He carried caution to the point of systematically refusing to say yes or no to any proposition whatever. "*C'est possible*" was as far as he was prepared to go.

A few days after I settled in I needed to ask him something or other. Like everyone else in the neighbourhood, of course, he knew perfectly well who I was. When you intrude on a small rural community you are fortunate if you can preserve your anonymity for longer than about ten minutes. Knowing what I did, I was certain that my impending arrival had been abundantly commented on and that the comments had been compounded of equal doses of curiosity and deep apprehension. As a matter of principle, Maxime was not prepared to let on that he had even heard of my existence. He remained unmoving at the door of his house as I approached, watching me with Cherokee impassivity.

"*Bon jour, Monsieur.* My name is Kershaw."

Dead silence followed while Maxime considered this claim. Finally, having made his mind up, he delivered judgement.

"*C'est possible.*"

He was incorrigible. He might be standing under torrential rain, for instance, but if I or anyone else mentioned that it was raining, Maxime, inscrutable as ever, would think it over and then, water streaming down his face, would concede, "*C'est possible.*"

When I got to know him, I would occasionally, although without much hope, try to force him to come into the open.

"How about buying me a drink, Maxime? It's my birthday."

"*C'est possible*".

"Listen, Maxime, it isn't possible, it isn't even just probable, it isn't guesswork, it's the simplest truth and you might just as well accept it."

"*C'est possible*".

By that stage I had become accustomed to this idioisyncracy of Maxime's. The first time I came up against it, however, I found it disconcerting, not to say frightening. That "*C'est possible.*" of his had me rattled. It sounded worse than merely noncommital, it was downright sceptical. I felt as if I had been caught using an alibi. The only other explanation that occurred to me was that I was suffering from some peculiar hallucination. Perhaps my name was not Kershaw at all? In which case, what was it? Who was I?

Even after it had been generally accepted that I was in fact called Kershaw, my name continued to cause difficulties. There are no k's or w's in French. A name which began with one and ended with the other was enough to make anyone suspicious. And the 'h' in the middle could not, by all the laws of God and the French Academy, be preceded by an 's'. Until we were on more familiar terms, my neighbours assailed me with all sorts of fugal variations on Kershaw: Kharkov, Kazakh, Kirghic; Khiva and Kvass were just a few of them. I was always a bit fearful that somebody, without wishing any harm, might come out with Monsieur Ketchup but, in the event, the worst that happened to me was to be addressed on one occasion as Monsieur Karloff and on another as Monsieur Kafka .

Apart from my unfortunate name, there was the problem of my nationality. Foreigners were not popular. And virtually everyone was a foreigner. Inhabitants of hamlets no more than a few hundred metres away were foreigners. So, in particular, were Parisians. The rare specimens who passed through were received, if they were received at all, with every sign of disgust. They were felt to have a condescending attitude towards countryfolk - which was true although three-quarters of them had most likely only migrated to the capital themselves ten or fifteen years earlier. Moreover, as in all the provinces of France, there was a deep-seated loathing for the post-revolutionary centralization of power. Paris was the source of every vexation which afflicted the rural community, from mildew to drought. All Parisians were universally believed to be spies in the pay of the taxation authorities or something worse. If there was anything worse.

During the Occupation a small number of German soldiers had been stationed nearby. Otherwise, not a soul in the the neighbourhood had ever seen a foreigner, no so much as an Englishman or an American, let alone a Pole, a Greek, a Swede, a Russian, a Swiss or a citizen of any other country than France . But it was known that the brutes existed and it was assumed that they were just like Germans, that they might be still more of a menace - determined sooner or later to invade the Republic spreading fire and rapine.

On the other hand, nobody had anything against Australians. Nobody had ever heard of us. We were about as well known as the Pitcairn Islanders. A handful of octogenarians had fought in the 1914-18 war and had some recollection of '*les Anzacs*' but as to where these Anzacs had come from, unless from a remote land called Anzacia, they were distinctly hazy. There was also an exceptionally bright lad in the village school who knew that Australia was an island. Somewhere in the Caribbean, he rather thought.

Returning from a week-end jaunt to Paris I got some idea of the extent of my neighbours' ignorance concerning the whereabouts of my native land. By that time it had been decided that there was no harm in talking to me and when I got back I was amiably questioned about what I had been up to. So how was everything in Australia? Good weather? Father and mother well? Aunts and uncles and cousins too? When it was discovered that I had spent the whole time in Paris the reaction was one of rather disapproving astonishment. With forty-eight hours to spare I could surely have whipped over to Australia1 possibly between lunch at the Coupole and dinner at the Closerie des Lilas. It was all too clear what everyone was thinking. These foreigners were an odd lot, no feeling for family ties at all.

Needless to say, I was initially treated with reserve on the grounds that I was not a native of the province. I was not even French although that would have done very little to improve my standing. Frenchmen from other regions were only minimally better than Italians or Portuguese. My nationality put me into a separate category. As an Australian, I became an object of interest, a curiosity, an inoffensive freak, midway between a village idiot and a two-headed calf. If there had been any tourists back then I would have rated as a tourist attraction. Compared to me, the various chateaux throughout the region wouldn't have had a hope of attracting any attention. It was a situation which suited me down to the ground. Far from objecting to the half-incredulous stares which I encountered, I considered myself fortunate. Better to be a two-headed calf any day than a Greek or a Swiss plotting to lay the country waste.

Topping off my eccentricities was the way I dressed, especially in summer when my thin cotton trousers, short-sleeved shirt and sandals provoked a combination of astonishment and commiseration. A miracle that I hadn't died of pneumonia! Normal peasant garb in those days consisted of corduroy trousers, a flannel vest, a thick shirt (sometimes two), a sweater, a waistcoat and a jacket. Berets were worn by one or two ancients but the usual headgear was a cloth cap, never removed indoors or out. Should the temperature drop below 25 C., a cummerbund might be added together with a scarf firmly knotted round the neck. When the heat became unendurable - more than 30 - it was deemed permissible, although a trifle foolhardy, to dispense with the scarf.

At our first meeting, that was how Maxime was dressed, cummerbund and all. An odd costume, I reflected, on what happened to be an especially warm spring day. But if he wanted to keel over with heat apoplexy that was his affair. What interested me was to see if I could somehow force him to say something, anything, apart from "C'est possible." There had to be some assertion I could make which he would be compelled to recognise as a plain statement of fact and not as a barely credible assertion with no evidence to support it.

"I ought to explain, Monsieur, that I've bought the house over the way."

"C'est possible."

This had me positively unnerved. I mean, I had bought the house, hadn't I? There wasn't any doubt, was there, that the previous owner had the right to sell? My God! Maybe there was a local ordinance forbidding the sale to anyone not engaged in agriculture. Did the house ever exist outside my imagination?

A quick check with the appropriate official department established that I had bought the house. So that was all right.. It was situated in what the French call a lieu-dit – a place known as" whatever it might be. A place known as is smaller than the smallest village - hamlet, I suppose, would be the nearest English equivalent.   There are hundreds, probably thousands of such minute conglomerations in France. No doubt they appear on the ordnance maps which show absolutely everything, down to tool sheds and sparrows' nests. They certainly won't be found on ordinary tourist maps, no matter how large the scale. Most *lieux-dit* have neither shops nor cafes. As far as my *lieu-dit* was concerned, there were no cars either, no tractors, no telephones and, blessedly, no radios.. Horses did the work of cars and tractors while local gossip conveyed the news of the day very much more rapidly and completely than radios and similar new-fangled   gadgets.

My place known as was a place known as Maison Salle.   I've no idea why and nobody could tell me. Nobody ever seemed lo ha ve an explanation for the peculiar names which dotted the countryside. Le *Gros* Poisson, for example - it would be fascinating to find out how many centuries ago he was caught (if he ever was caught) and just how gros he was. Any fish that had a village named after it must have been a whopper. Then there is Saint Satur not far away. Who was Saint *Satur*? Heaven knows or, at any rate, in the matter of saints ought to know. But I'm not sure that even heaven could identify this one. Could it be derived Satur - it sounds vaguely pagan. from Saturn or perhaps from satyr?

As to Maison Salle, the only solution I ever heard offered was that there had once been a house on the site belonging to a family called Salle. Unhappily, the local archives contained no indication that any such family had ever existed. Not that I dug very deeply because, strictly speaking, I didn't belong to Maison Salle anyway. A narrow unmetalled road separated my house from the others. The opposite side of the road was Maison Salle. On my side, according to the cadastral map, my family and I were the sole inhabitants of a place called Tayaux. To have my own personal, private hamlet was an intoxicating notion. I saw myself as a sort of feudal overlord with the right to exercise the high, the middle and the low justice. Unhappily, no-one apart from the makers of the cadastral map had ever heard of Tayaux so that to use it as my address would have puzzled the postman among others. Reluctantly, therefore, I resigned myself to being a plain resident of Maison Salle like everyone else.

Why Tayaux was called Tayaux I never found out either. One suggestion which I heard was that Tayaux was a corruption of ta aut! - tally-ho! - and since a forest not far off had always been plentifully supplied with deer and wild boar, that sounded plausible enough and I didn't bother to carry my researches any further.

At least I learnt why our nearest village was called Sury-en-Vaux, which was also the name of the *commune* encompassing Maison Salle and Tayaux. Sury-en-Vaux was a deformation of Le Sourie dans les Valldes - The Smile in the Valleys. Parisian tourists were inclined to giggle at what they considered to be a sentimental and over-poetic designation. Personally, I thought it admirably apposite. The most supercilious tourist could hardly deny that the village was situated in one of the numerous valleys of the district. And seeing it from the vine-covered slopes which surrounded it, the atmosphere of unalterable tranquility somehow suggested that Sury-en-Vaux really was smiling quietly to itself, that it really was the smile in the valleys. For the disdainful tourists, it was almost a caricature, a picture-postcard village, with its cluster of ancient houses round the church and the communal well on the edge of its tiny square. A block of workers' flats and a neon-lit drug store might have made it more acceptable to the tourists. Not to me.

Maison Salle was some ten or twelve kilometres south of the Loire, in the ancient province of the Berry. I was the only one of its fifteen inhabitants who was not a peasant. I was also the only one unable to speak the Berrichon *patois.* That did nothing to make things easier for me. Words were pronounced as they had been in the 16th century. All sorts of local terms and phrases not to be found in any standard dictionary added to my bewilderment. It was a long time before I contributed much more to any conversation than a nod or a shake of the head, hoping without much confidence that I had not nodded when I should have shaken or shaken when a nod would have been appropriate.

The *garde, en-garde* around the vines of Sury-en-Vaux.

One of the main reasons for buying a house was to provide a refuge for an old friend who was deep in financial trouble. He was no longer young and at best had never been notably efficient in dealing with practical matters. I could not see him lighting fires or kerosene lamps or taking a bath in a tub of water which he had drawn from a well. That meant finding a place with electricity, central heating, running water, a bathroom.

Modern conveniences common in rural France as of this kind were then about as caviar for breakfast. I visited dozens of houses. They were picturesque. Some of them had electricity. That was a if had clearly been installed by the bit too picturesque local blacksmith after an imperfectly understood reading of a do-it-yourself manual. I could not get rid of the notion that at any moment the garlands of naked wires looped overhead would come in contact and the whole place would burst into flames. In any case, there was no running water. Others could offer running water but no electricity. None of them possessed either central heating or bathrooms.

Picturesque was not the word to describe the house I finally located and (however many doubts Maxime chose to sow in my mind as to the legality of the sale) bought. It was an unappealing modern edifice, the only building within miles less than a hundred years older and certain features of its construction suggested that it had been designed by an exhausted Soviet functionary in the employment of Gosplan. The windows on the first floor suffered from a fairly basic defect which would have made any Muscovite feel right at home. They were traversed by heavy bean so that it was impossible to open them. Not that one wasted any time in trying to open them since the loony designer had omitted to put in a staircase. Access to the upper storey could only be effected by oozing through a hatch in the garage ceiling and scrambling over wooden slats bestrewn with the broken bottles left behind by the builders.

My wife and a friend skilled in such operations eventually succeeded in transforming it until it could be contemplated without revulsion. They even made it reasonably attractive. My first sight of it, however, was discouraging. At least, I told myself desperately, it was unpretentious. If it had had the insolence to try and be pretentious, I think I might have set fire to it. And, struggling to find a silver lining, I noted that at any rate the electrical installation did not induce a nervous trembling, the running water ran, there was central heating and a bathroom with a bath in it.

I had indulged in a sentimental fancy that the house I eventually found would be surrounded by an old-world garden. I imagined myself sniffing at honeysuckle of a morning, possibly pruning apple trees and eradicating slugs from the midst of the hollyhocks. There was no old world garden. The house stood uncompromisingly in the middle of a paddock. Rank dishevelled grass three feet high sprouted where I had tenderly envisaged trailing wistaria, herbaceous borders, foxgloves and snapdragons. One waded through a glutinous mire to reach the door.

By way of compensation, there were the vine-covered hills on all sides. That clinched the matter as far as I was concerned. Drinking wine in a hot bath while exulting in electric light and listening to the gurgle of the radiators - it seemed to me that if the old friend for whom the house was intended couldn't be happy in such circumstances then there was no pleasing him. I did a certain amount of deft borrowing here and there and the house was mine. It had six rooms. The neighbours, however, awed by its central heating and electricity, referred to it admiringly as "the chateau".

Furnishing it was no problem. There were two carpenters in the nearby village. M. Bizet could claim that his family had been carpenters from father to son since the 17th century. This was quite true, I discovered. The records were on file in the village hall. It may have been on account of his distinguished lineage that his prices were somewhat higher than those of his competitor, M. Vattan. I chose M. Vattan.

It was the right choice, I discovered. His work may not have been quite as finished as that of M. Bizet but this, in my view, was offset by his engaging reluctance to present his modest bills. One got the impression that he considered there was something distasteful about any mention of money.

The first thing he made for me was a table - solid oak without a nail or a screw in it - for a price agreed on in advance, and a very reasonable price at that. A week or so after it was delivered, I went on call on him.

"Good morning, M.. Vattan, I've come to pay my debts."

"Ah, but M. Kharkov, I haven't had time to make out the bill."

"That's of no importance, M. Vattan. We agreed on the price, I think?"

"Of course, of course, M. Kazakh. But you must have the bill first. We must be business-like, *nest-ce pas*?"

"I assure you, I don't need a bill, M. Vattan. Nor a receipt. Here's the money."

"Some other time. M. Kirghiz – when I've made out the bill. *Tiens*, 11 o'clock. What do you say to a glass of wine?"

Over the next twelve months or so, I made repeated calls on M. Vattan, imploring him to take the money I owed him. They always ended up the same way, with M. Vattan leading me firmly to the cellar, the debt still unpaid. After a while, I no longer anticipated that he would ever allow me to settle it. My visits became a formality more than anything else.

"About the money I owe you M. Vattan... "

"Some other time, *cher Monsieur*, some other time. When I've made out the bill. You haven't tried the new wine?, have you?" Off we went to the cellar.

When he finally accepted payment, I was slightly put out. I'd come to think that we were on purely social terms. I consoled myself with the thought that the money I handed across must have barely covered the cost of the wine I was given whenever I called.

Most of my encounters in the early days were of a purely commercial nature and took place in Sury-en-Vaux. Since I had not had the effrontery to make my home in Sury, I was accepted somewhat more readily there than in my adopted hamlet. As in the case of my dealings with M. Vattan, all transactions were invariably accompanied by a glass or two of wine, as much a ritual as the offer of a cup of coffee among Turks and Arabs. Everybody, whether or not he was a professional *vigneron*, had a few vines of his own and made a certain amount of wine. And everybody could spare the time to drink some of it. The purchase of a kilo of potatoes or a leg of lamb was a ceremony. A little urbane conversation, wholly unconnected with the business of buying and selling, was the first step.

"Do you know what I just saw on my way here, M. Boin? A very nasty-looking adder."

"Let me tell you something, M. Korchov. There are worse things than adders. Hornets. My uncle Leon was stung by a hornet in 1940. He seemed to be all right but only five years later - no, six - he died. Another three months and he would have been eighty-eight. The hornet had weakened his constitution, you see. *C'est pour vous dire*."

"Perhaps he wasn't given the right treatment."

"Ah, but he was, *cher Monsieur*. A hot poultice of willow leaves and spring onions macerated in red wine. There's no better treatment for hornet stings. And talking of wine, what do you say to a glass?"

Yes was the answer to that. A refusal would have soured relations for ever. The eggs or whatever it might be could wait. Any other customers who happened to turn up while we were in the cellar knew where to find us and glasses would be awaiting them, too.

A baker's, a butcher's and a general store made up the shopping facilities in Sury. For anything else, one had to climb up to the lovely little hill town of Sancerre. Conviviality was the rule there, too. It was the Sancerre greengrocer who took me down to his magnificent 18th-century vaulted cellar one memorable day. The occasion is firmly fixed in my memory because, on a glacial winter morning, he served slices of cold raw blood pudding with the wine. I was rightly proud of myself for managing to gobble them up with suitable cries of ecstacy.

Cold blood pudding is not the only reason why that particular occasion has stuck in my mind. It was the same day that I established myself as a wit of uncommon drollery. Leaving the hospitable greengrocer, I met our *garde champetre* a combination of official gamekeeper, village policeman (he wore a kepi but had no powers of arrest) and messenger boy for the mayor's office in Sury-en-Vaux. That we should have run into each other so far from home - a good six or seven kilometres - was an event. He hailed me, I thought, with relief. Exiled among the alien Sancerrois, he was obviously enchanted to see a familiar face.

" M. Karshev! What brings you to the metropolis?"

"Just marketing, M. le Garde."

"I came to deliver a paper – an official paper, you understand - at the town hall. So here you are and here am I. You know what I think? I think it calls for a glass of wine. What do you say?"

"What do I say, M. le Garde? I say it's indispensable."

To this day, I can't imagine why the *garde champetre* should have found my reply so irresistibly comic. He did, though. Doubled up, gyrating wildly and waving his arms about in uncontrollable delight, it was some time before he could utter a word. When he had recovered, "*Eh, oui.*" He said between renewed spasms, "*Vous l'avez bien dit – c'est indispensable!* Indispensable - that's the word all right!" While we were drinking our wine in the nearest cafe, the *garde* would every so often put down his glass to erupt in a further paroxysm. "*Ah, ca alors, c'est le cas de le dire, c'est indispensable!*"

Official business seemed to oblige the *garde* to spend much of his time in one of the village cafes. Whenever I dropped in myself for an aperitif, he would leer at me as though we shared some faintly improper secret. Then, the leer expanding into a joyous smile, he would nudge me slyly in the ribs. "*Alors, M. Karchev – c'est indispensable, nein?*" And he would go off into a prolonged spasm of hilarity.

Once, when I had lent the house to some friends, I urged them to look in at the cafe. They could count on finding the *garde* there, I told them. "Just say, '*Bonjour, le Garde*, don't you think it's indispensable?' and watch his reaction". They followed my instructions. Hearing the magic word, the garde guffawed ecstatically, sputtered, choked and flapped his arms for several minutes. Then, "You needn't tell me", he said, "you're friends of M. Kikhav, no doubt about that. Oh, yes, it's indispensable all right! And for me it's a *pastis* that's indispensable. What about you, Messieurs? *Ah, qu'il est drole, ce cher M. Koklev!* No, but how about it, eh? That's the word, no? Indispensable!" And he collapsed all over again.

ROUND ONE

We are living, the whole lot of us, in the joyless age. The Lord Protector and his accomplices were roisterers and roaring boys by comparison with the "causists" (since I don't know what else to call the hysterical zealots who plague us these days), the impudent politicians, the hyperactive bureaucrats and all the other self-assertive pests who tell us what we must and mustn't do. Drunkeness is high on their list of reprehensible practices. Psychiatrists and psycho-analysts - wowsers under the skin - go scampering after the causes of excessive drinking and come up with hilariously absurd answers. That there might be people who drink too much because they like it is the only explanation that these lugubrious know-alls refuse to consider. The social misfits (the rest of us) may think they're enjoying themselves but in reality, according tothe witch-doctors squatting beside the captive booby's couch at 100 an hour, they are sufferers, to be saved at all costs (at their own cost, that is), they have a "drink problem". Who but the psycho-wowsers would have so determinedly set about transforming a pleasure into a problem?

Speaking for my fellow sots and myself, the one overwhelming problem we had to contend with was how to get enough to pay for the next round. Apart from that, we hadn't any problems at all. That was what made us peculiarly obnoxious in the eyes not merely of the analysts, psychiatrists, psychologists and similar humbugs but, even more, in the eyes of politicians and sociologists. The latter have appointed themselves custodians of the utilitarian side of things. Alcohol, they point out with a shaking of heads and a wagging of fingers, lowers our productivity and gives rise to anti-social impulses. Indeed it does, thank God. But suppposing we want our productivity to be lowered, lowered to vanishing point? And supposing that anti social impulses are the sort of impulses we like best? Then it becomes not just a transcendental pleasure to drink, to drink too much, too often, but a solemn duty in the fulfilment of which we can take pride. Unless we are resigned to becoming social milch cows or drably "good citizens", drunkeness is one way - and may soon be the only way - in which we can affirm that we are free men. Let every hiccup be a cry of defiance and every belch a challenge! We must sacrifice our livers for the sake of life.

This, for what it's worth, is my theme. If I only had the necessary talent, of course, I would try to write one of those forbidding "encyclopaedias"of wines and spirits. That's where the money is. Unhappily, I not only lack the talent but also the self-assurance. Somehow I wouldn't feel easy about issuing those injunctions and prohibitions which apparently are just what the readers expect and pay for. The authors of these compilations are just as keen as the sociologists, the psychologists, the bureaucrats and the rest of them to tell us what we are permitted to like and what we'd do well to shun. Myself, I don't need any help, and still less any orders, in deciding what I enjoy. And this is a book about enjoyment.

Then there are the apologists for drinking. They are almost as exasperating as the wowsers. Instead of frankly admitting that they like alcohol as a joyous affirmation of life, they carry on like so many Reverend Stigginses. They take care to be shamefaced, conciliatory, as though some principle, moral or therapeutic, needed to be invoked in order to justify a glass of beer or a noggin of rum. Take old Robert Burton, for example, in his Anatomy of Melancholy. You'd think he was prescribing a patent medicine.

Drink is a most easy and parable remedy, a common, a cheap, still ready against fear, sorrow and such troublesome thoughts, that molest the mind; as brimstone with fire, the spirits on a sudden are enlightened by it.

My friends and I were young. We never thought of drink as a parable remedy. We didn't need one. Our minds were never molested by troublesome thoughts. Probably we could be imprisoned for it today but we enjoyed life and hence we enjoyed drunkeness for its own delectable sake.

No, give me Dean Aldrich any day in preference to Burton. The Dean (and I hope he rose to even greater ecclesiastical eminence) spoke out for drinking in lines which I'd like to see branded on every sociological and psychoanalytical forehead.

If all be true that I do think,
There are five reasons we should drink:
Good wine - a friend - or being dry -
Or lest we should be by and by -
Or any other reason why.

Now that's what I call good commonsense. My only objection (supposing I wanted to make one) is that there seems to be a hint in the Dean's quintain that drink means wine and only wine. If so, I'd have to argue with him. There was never anything exclusive in the drinking habits of my companions and myself. We shunned water, naturally, and water-drinkers likewise.

But what are these that from the outer murk
Of dense mephitic vapours creeping lurk
To breathe foul airs from that corrupted well
Which oozes slime along the floors of Hell?
These are the stricken palsied brood of sin
In whose vile veins, poor, poisonous and thin,
Decoctions of embittered hatreds crawl:
These are the Water-Drinkers, cursed all!

Apart from water (and milk and lemonade) we were prepared to drink anything liquid. And, in my own case, apart from gin unless it was the Plymouth gin which outmatches any German or Dutch schnapps and has none of the distressing side-effects of the so-called London type. I experienced those side-effects with devastating completeness at a party given by a group of medical students. That was a memorable do. It took place in an East Melbourne loft to which you ascended by means of a steep ladder. You were supposed to descend by the same means. Not everyone did. When, finally, the neighbours called the police and we were all ordered out, half the guests stumbled across the room, missed the top rung and cascaded into the lane below. There was quite a heap of them in the end. As each one landed, I burst into tears. I'd like to pretend that this was in consequence of my nice compassionate nature. The truth is, however, that I'd been bursting into tears intermittently throughout the evening. If only I'd followed the example of one of the revellers who with impressive aplomb picked up and drank formaldehyde or some similar dissecting-room fluid. Instead, I'd been drinking gin, gin that wasn't Plymouth gin. I've usually managed to take a charitable view of my own misbehaviour but I remember with shame the effect that that gin had on me. It induced a Slavic despondency of such intensity that whenever anyone spoke to me I started caterwauling. It didn't matter what was said.

"What did you think of So-and-So's new paintings?"

"Wah, wah!"

"I must remember to give you back that book you lent me."

"Boo-hoo!"

That was the last time I drank gin.

For the rest, a gleeful over-indulgence in rum, whisky, wine, beer, not to mention a number of rare compounds which I'll be mentioning in due course, always led me, ramblingly, to Prospero's cell or the Kingdom of Micomicon or the palace of Prester John. It didn't matter whether I was reeling along with my head in the stars and my feet in the gutter or my head in the gutter and my feet in the stars, whether I was talking to a cow in the middle of a field or to a blank wall in the middle of the city, it didn't matter if cars were missing me by inches or even not missing me (I was catapulted about ten feet one night on the Boulevard Montparnasse) - whatever the circumstances mysterious revelations would explode within me like fireworks.

I know more than Apollo
For when the world is sleeping
I watch the stars
Of mortal wars
In the wounded welkin weeping

That was me, all right. I knew more than Apollo, every time. And each individual hangover seemed well worthwhile. I abandoned drugs almost as soon as I'd sampled them. Opium gave me nothing but a sore throat.

Cocaine didn't even give me that. Marijuana was all right, I suppose, but it wasn't a patch on arack or mare or, as I discovered in Herefordshire, rough cider off the wood.

A long jump had to be made between Melbourne and Herefordshire but it was in Melbourne that the pilgrimage began. There was a modish, not to say roguish, tobacco shop at the top end of Collins Street in the days before smoking became a misdemeanour. A few of us were devout aesthetes, worshippers of Wilde and Huysmans: at seventeen, you have to be a devout something or other. The Collins Street bower was the only tobacco shop which we felt to be exquisite enough to deserve our custom. It purveyed some notably exotic items. Our preference was for its own brand of cigarette, a slender tube of black paper with a gold tip. Now, what could one drink as an accompaniment to anything as wonderfully effete as that? Not beer, obviously. Beer, we told each other shudderingly, was better suited to football crowds. You might almost say it was the embodiment of a football crowd - blatant, unsubtle and plain boisterous.

We chose some conspicuously horrible decoctions as being the sort of thing Lord Henry Wotton or Des Esseintes would have favoured. One in particular, I remember, was a lilac-coloured liqueur called Parfait Amour. It smelt of patchouli and the taste was like a concentrate of Turkish Delight. I dare say, if you'd seen us, you would have sneered at our affectations. But even as you sneered you would have had to recognise that, aesthetes or not, we were a courageous bunch. Swallowing Parfait Amour took some doing in itself. And you had to be downright foolhardy to order it in an Australian pub of the Thirties.

***

It's unseemly to quote from one's own writings: but in a book I published a few years ago I reminisced about those pubs and I think the description has its place here:

They were the closest thing to lazar-houses since the Middle Ages. You took your life in your hands whenever you ordered a beer. It was good beer but the way it was served was something you had to get accustomed to. I doubt if anyone ever had the nerve to ask for a clean glass. You might just as well have worn a green carnation in your buttonhole and be done with it. You got the glass used by the previous drinker, the stale suds still clinging to its sides. As a concession to customers' finicky prejudices, it might be dipped briefly into a dank tarn of cold water before being refilled but that was the most you could expect. I 'II never know why we didn't all go down with Tapanuli Fever or the Black Formosan Corruption.

Towards the end of the day came the really ghoulish part. Pubs closed at six sharp. The wage-slaves emerged from offices and factories at five. That gave them one hour in which to slake thirsts that took a lot of slaking. By ten past five, a bawling concourse of single-minded citizens was lined up atthe counter, seven, eight, nine deep. There was no more namby-pamby rinsing of glasses. Speed was what counted. Glasses were emptied in one stupendous gulp, passed over intervening heads to the bar, refilled and passed back. By ten to six everyone was hoarse, good and drunk, and looking for a fight. That was the moment to make your getaway. If you were quick enough on your feet you might escape without somebody being sick over your shoes.

Not that the old pubs were without merit. Even in our most decadent phase, I think we relished their sheer ruffianism, they had a Klondike reek to them. You felt that at any moment, someone might pay for drinks with (a bag of gold dust or shoot the barman. There was some rich poetry produced there, too. "Give us a beer, mate - I'm as dry as a dead dingo's dong" was one utterance that I thought and still think was both resonant and imaginative. And I had a tenderness for a phrase (not to be found in the Australian National Dictionary, to my astonishment) which was used whenever one of us was overheard to make some offensively pretentious remark. On such occasions, one of the less refined drinkers would be sure to mutter, "Duck the skull!", a shorthand version of "Duck the skull, the bullshit's flying".

I often wonder how we Parfait Amour drinkers were allowed to get away with it. Come to that, what was anything as dainty as Parfait Amour doing in Australian pubs? I doubt you could have got a Benedictine, say, or a Cointreau back then. So how did Parfait Amour come to be on the shelves? The only explanation I can find is that all those brawny truck-drivers and football fans were in the habit of taking a surreptitious swig of the stuff when nobody was looking.

ROUND TWO

'I rather like bad wine,' said Mr Mountchesney, 'one gets so bored with good wine.'

Wilde had taught us that man did not live by Parfait Amour alone. Wine, too, was an essential element in the aesthetic life. The Master's work was full of luscious evocations of "amber-coloured" champagne and similar glamorous goodies. Champagne was beyond our means and what Australia had to offer as an alternative was not enticing. The admirable vintages to be had nowadays didn't exist then. Australian wine was an acquired taste and anyone who didn't acquire it could consider himself lucky.

In Carlton, I think it was, a man called Jimmy Watson dispensed what were supposed to be the best local wines available. Maybe they were but they all seemed pretty acrid to me. No doubt I was wrong. If ever there was an unrefined palate it was mine. In the end, my friends and I settled for a viscid potion which, from fear of reprisals, I won't identify. It wasn't exactly amber-coloured, more a goose-turd green. It oozed from its fancy bottle with all the gay effervescence of sump oil. Disraeli's Mr Mountchesney would have loved it.

Later on, we abandoned the Nineties for the Twenties and switched to cocktails. But we were still aesthetic enough to abjure the more astringent varieties, Martinis and what-not.

We went in for - I can't even recall the names but maraschino, icing-sugar and, for all I know, marshmallows and chocolate fudge, entered largely into their composition. We also favoured a witch's brew called Avocaat which was largely compounded of eggs and looked not so much like something to drink as something which had already been drunk and promptly regurgitated. In our Twenties phase, we smoked our gold-tipped cigarettes in foot-long holders. Looking back, I'm baffled as to why we weren't set upon by the stalwart fellows swigging their schooners besides us.

And so, by slow degrees, we progressed to beer.

A character in Norman Lindsay's *Redheap* summed up our view of beer.

'Look it up in the dictionary, and what do you find? A liquor extracted from malt and flavoured with hops. Rot! It is a tincture of eternity, extracted from light, and distilled by man. On the authority of Plato, it is that essence which holds the universe together. It holds us together. Whether you take it from the sun or a bottle is a mere pedantic idiosyncrasy. In either case, you take it.'

That was how we looked at it - beer held us together. It was, in any case, what we'd really wanted all along but, with Wilde and Dowson and Verlaine and, later on, Noel Coward and the rest of them keeping an eye on us, we hadn't had the nerve to admit it.

Australian beer was great stuff back then. It wasn't ale as found in Saxon rumkins, it wasn't nut-brown. It was a buoyant lager-type of beer with a redoubtable kick to it. And it wasn't soporific like German beer or insignificant like French beer or staid like English beer. It was unique. I was surprised when I visited one of the breweries and found myself surrounded by a glitteringly macabre decor which might have been a nuclear power station. I'd always imagined that Australian beer was brewed by carefree gnomes in underground caverns.

The pre-eminent beer-drinker among us was Deasey, infatuated with his Irish ancestry and resolved to preserve the crapulous reputation of the Old Country. He became more Hibernian with each gulp, bawling insults at the other drinkers in a brogue thicker than anything ever heard in Connemara. I doubt if he could have held his own with a reasonably skilled bantamweight but he was large enough to be intimidating and the drinkers he picked on usually backed off.

By the time we were evicted at six o'clock, the pugnacious phase would have been succeeded by a mystic yearning to go from anywhere to anywhere at incalculable speeds. For this purpose he had at his disposal a massive car which even when merely limbering up emitted a menacing rumble and which, once it got going, shot through time and space like an asteroid. All too often I was persuaded to accompany Deasey on these maniacal jaunts of his.

On one such occasion we went roaring off to some country pub where the boss was said to regard - and rightly - six o'clock closing as a monstrous infringement of the rights of man. We drank deeply with him. After an hour or two of swigging and swilling, "It's blind I am", mumbled Deasey, more than ever like something direct from the Abbey Theatre. Well, I was blind myself; only it turned out that Deasey meant he really was blind - at any rate, he couldn't see anything except a roseate blur. "So it's up to you, me boyo, to get us back to Melbourne Town."

"What are you talking about, Deasey? You know damn well I can't drive."

"And would ye be making a fuss about a tiny thing

like that, now? It's talkin' like a spineless Orangeman ye are, bad cess to ye. All I'm askin' of you is to take the wheel on account of me troubled vision. As to the pedals and levers, it's meself will take charge of them." Stark madness can seem like sweet reasonableness when you've had enough to drink. Straight away I realised that Deasey had found the solution. I installed myself at the wheel and off we went. Nothing to it. I twiddled the wheel like a champion. Beside me, Deasey lay back with eyes firmly closed. He sang most of the time. We had "The Wearing of the Green" and "Molly Malone" and "The Shan Van Voght". Now and again, without opening his eyes, he manipulated those levers and pedals. We got to the edge of the city without a scratch. Then we both passed out.

We were, as I've tried to convey, a vulgarly cheerful lot. But whenever we drank beer we seemed to be overtaken by an irrepressible desire to commit suicide out of sheer *joie de vivre*, you might say. When we weren't being catapulted along in Deasey' scar, we would go swimming, usually around three o'clock in the morning. By all the rules, we should have been instantaneously seized with cramp or congestion of the lungs or something of the sort. Or we might have been taken by sharks. At least once, if any of them had been around, they could have made a significant difference to the history of Australian art. Bert Tucker and Arthur Boyd, I think, and certainly Sid Nolan were among those splashing about off Frankston or Black Rock one bibulous night. A single snap of the jaws and we'd never have had the Ned Kelly series. A sobering thought, that.

***

And, no matter who's paying, tell me a better way of wearing down a bright and sultry morning, when the rest of the world is stamping itself silly with work, than by ambling, skidding or glissading in chromatic progressions from bar to bar ...

We may not have been able to match Adrian Lawlor, that sublime fantast and scandalously gifted artist,

in any other respect; but he couldn't tell us anything about the delight of pub-crawling.

Pubs were all over Melbourne in those days and you rarely had to crawl more than a hundred yards to get from one to another. Some of the pubs Adrian and I knew were frequented by journalists, others by corduroyed painters, some were the watering holes of barristers and some were more or less the reserve of sports fans. We weren't choosy in the matter. As long as the beer was good (and my ramshackle memory insists that it always was) we were happy in any of them.

It was unthinkable, though, to linger unduly in one particular pub. The crawl, or as Adrian more elegantly put it, the glissading in chromatic progressions, was as important as the beer. We were sworn enemies of asceticism but there was what you might call a bitter-sweet pleasure to be had from foregoing the extra glass we so badly wanted and staggering on our way with voluptuous visions of the glass awaiting us at the next stop.

ROUND THREE

And all the time we stayed faithful to our belief that the only way to drink was to drink too much. Our models were the "decent people of Lichfield" described by Dr Johnson, who "got drunk every night". But Johnson notes that they "were not the worse thought of'. That wouldn't have suited us at all. We wanted to be thought the worse of. Our great ambition was to shock the bourgeoisie. Unfortunately, the burgesses didn't even notice us. Occasionally we might be invited to leave a pub - the invitation, if you can call it that, usually consisting of a bellowed, "Get out of here, yer bloody drongoes" - and occasionally an ill dispositioned cop would direct a warning scowl at us but that was as far as it went. We had to be content with telling ourselves what reprobates we were. Then one of us came on Nimrod's life of Squire Mytton with its description of the Squire's drinking habits and we realised that we still had a long way to go. Four to six bottles of port wine was apparently the Squire's minimum daily consumption. We knew we could never equal that. Reading about the Squire's intake certainly forced us to re-assess our own capacities but we went on bragging untruthfully to each other about how much we'd put down the previous day. By way of variation, we would let it be known that delirium tremens was just around the corner unless we got to a bottle fast.

A film depicting an alcoholic's desperate efforts to get a drink provided us with a role which we played with enthusiasm. We were all given to play-acting but our friend Max Harris was perhaps better at it than the rest of us. The film inspired him. Somehow concealing the fact that he was almost sickeningly healthy and that his energy was limitless, he was to be seen for weeks after emerging from the cinema weaving erratically along the street, unshaven and with a tendency to stumble from time to time. Sometimes he carried his neo-realistic artistry to the point of actually collapsing on the ground and grazing his knees. Every so often, having made sure that someone was watching, he would pull a flask from his pocket and take an anguished gulp of whatever it was. It was no use trying to compete with him. His facial tics and nervous tremblings of the hands were perfect theatre ...

It must have been Max's virtuoso performance which directed our attention to spirits.

Oh some are for the lily, and some are for the rose,
But I am for the sugar-cane that in Jamaica grows,
For it's that that makes the bonny drink to warm
 my copper nose,
Says the old bold mate of Henry Morgan.

Masefield should have known better than to ascribe such an absurd taste to a decent sailorman. Metrically, it might have been a bit tricky substituting Queensland for Jamaica but when poetry comes into conflict with the taste buds, poetry must yield. I suppose Stevenson's Billy Bones who pronounced himself "a poor old hulk on a lee-shore" if deprived of rum also went in for the pernicious Jamaican product. They didn't know what they were missing, the pair of them. If they could only have sampled a genuine Bunderberg rum!

I'm not much subject to blasts of moral outrage. Quite recently, however, a work called The Earnest Drinker' Digest managed to provoke me to pulpit-hammering frenzy. Rum, says the author (an Australian, too, believe. it or not), is made in - and he lists the birthplaces: Jamaica, Barbados, Demerara, Trinidad, Martinique, Guadeloupe, Porto Rico and Guiana. "Good rum", he adds offllandedly, "is also made in Queensland (Australia)".

What is made in Queensland (Australia) is not " good", it is not even very good. It is the ultimate rum, it is the ideal to which all other rums vainly aspire. The demon rum? Maybe; but, if so, the demon is a friendly demon, a demon with outstretched hand, a sublime demon, Lucifer, son of the morning.

Don't take this for gross chauvinism. The idiotic carrying on about "national identity" is among the least endearing traits which my besotted countrymen have developed and I want no part of it. But truth is truth; and I can produce witnesses to prove that my judgement is as objective as anyone could ask. Living in France, I have occasionally poured a small, a very small glass (after all it's not easy to come by in France) of overproof Queensland rum for my friends. Their response has invariably been one of simple wonder. Brought up since childhood in the belief that only France produces potable spirits, they have begun by hinting that this incomparable rum, although hitherto unknown to them, must have been distilled in some remote comer of the Jura or the Auvergne. Forced to admit that sugar-cane would have a hard time of it in the sub-zero temperatures which prevail in those regions in winter, they have suggested that what I was offering must have come from *la France d'outre-mer* - Tahiti, say, or New Caledonia. "Australia", they would mutter when finally persuaded that I was telling the truth, "must be a magnificent country".

The great rum of Bunderberg was beyond our means except when one or another of us was unexpectedly flush. Mostly we had to content ourselves with beer although that was no hardship. Beer or ale? Which was it we drank? I've never bothered to find out the technical difference, if there is one, between the two. Ale sounds somehow more alluring than beer - all those poems about ale in a Saxon rumkin and jolly good ale and old and good ale thou art my darling. One way or another I had to taste this ale that the balladeers made such a fuss about. I won't say that I headed for England as soon as the war was over for the sole purpose of sampling it but during the interminable voyage it was never far from my mind. Especially because I was travelling on a ship which was to all appearances an unconverted prison hulk. The captain was a fairly psychotic madcap with an uncertain talent for navigation (he ran us aground at one point) and a powerful conviction that it was up to him to maintain discipline among the cowed passengers. We never saw him. We used to hear him, though, constantly, when he bellowed orders, reprimands and, now and again, plain invective through the public address system. The bunks were as comfortable to sleep on as a wasps' nest. The food was unrecognisable as anything known to science.

All this could have been home if one had had access to strong liquor. But that was among the prohibitions enacted by the captain. There wasn't going to be any merrymaking on his ship, we could make up our minds to that.

What shall we do with a drunken sailor,
What shall we do with a drunken sailor,
What shall we do with a drunken sailor,
Early in the morning?

Early in the morning or in the middle of the night, I know what I would have done. I would have fallen on my knees imploring him to tell me how he had managed to get drunk on that gruesome vessel. There were no drunken sailors that I ever saw. Come to think of it, I don't remember ever seeing a sailor of any kind, drunk or sober. Perhaps there weren't any. It may have been a ghost ship. That would account for a lot.

The painter James Gleeson was aboard. He was not travelling first class because there wasn't any but in a class somewhat superior to the "steerage" in which we were pigging it. He was even entitled to buy drink and would occasionally risk being put in irons by the mad captain and smuggle a glass to me. No friendship could have had a happier beginning. He could not, however, provide me with enough to calm my thirst.

For six weeks as we moved sluggishly towards England I kept brooding on that ale.

Ship me somewheres east of Suez, where the best is like the worst,
Where there ain't no Ten Commandments, an' a man can raise a thirst.

Kipling might have had me in mind. Is Aden east of Suez? It sounds as if it ought to be. Anyway, that's where I'd been shipped to and I'd certainly raised a thirst, an incandescent thirst, by the time I got there.

A disheartening place, Aden. If there was any vegetation around, I don't recall it. The temperature must have been in the vicinity of 45 C and the sun lurked obscurely behind a hellish black sky that seemed to be fixed forever about six feet over our heads. There was nothing resembling a pub or a cafe at the dock side. Still it was wonderful to be allowed off that frightful ship of ours. The captain didn't even send an armed escort to keep an eye on us. For a few hours we were free.

There were half a dozen decrepit taxis waiting. We piled into one of them and asked to be taken to the centre of town. Exuding murderous hatred of the Roum, the driver took off at Deaseyish speed. We came to a ramshackle collection of huts. The centre of town? The driver gave a sort of affirmative snarl. We had to take his word for it. One of the huts housed a sinister-looking cafe. I think the proprietor must have been the driver's brother. They had the same sunny disposition. Sweat pouring down our faces, we ordered beer. No beer, the proprietor told us with evident satisfaction. Wine? No wine. Rum and water? No rum. The proprietor was having a lovely time reciting all the things he hadn't got. So what, in God's name, could we have? This was the moment the proprietor had been waiting for. His eyes glittering with ill-will, Benedictine, he told us, we could have Benedictine. We drank it, of course - there was nothing else to do. At 45 in the shade or whatever it was, drinking Benedictine was an unspeakable experience.

In his reminiscences that old soak Norman Douglas gives an account of his twenty-first birthday party. He and his friends, he explains, got so stinking drunk that they boiled tinned lobsters in Benedictine and then ate the lobsters and drank the Benedictine. Until I got to Aden I'd always thought that that performance represented the ultimate in horror. I was wrong. Douglas at least drank his Benedictine in Paris, in winter. I drank mine in Aden, at the hottest time of the year. That was quite astesting an experience as adding a lobster flavouring to one's drink.

ROUND FOUR

It was a disappointment, the jolly good ale and old, when I finally reached England. The macabre voyage with the bellowing captain, all six weeks of it, was over, was over, was over, and I disembarked from the hellship exultantly except for a feeling that at any moment the press gang might be after me. An Australian friend was waiting for me and we drove away from Southampton through the English countryside. Spring that year was spectacular, like a green bushfire, but I thought I could postpone any Wordsworthian raptures until I'd had a drink. Ale in a Saxon rumkin! We stopped at the first pub we came to.

My notion of what an English pub ought to be like came from passages here and there in Dickens and this one seemed to be a thorough-going Dickensian tavern if ever there was one. Sporting prints and a couple of hunting horns on the walls, dark beams, rows of pewter mugs - it was all very encouraging. Tom Brown's Schooldays had made an impression, too. I remembered aslavering enumeration of the breakfast dishes served at one particular inn - pigeon-pie was one item, and ham, cold boiled beef, kidneys, steaks, bacon, poached eggs, toast, muffins ... And to drink, of course, there was that jolly good ale.

But William IV, unhappily, was no longer on the throne. The England I came to was occupied territory, ruled by a Socialist government which held this truth to be self-evident that all men might not be born equal but that they could certainly, under duress, be made equal - equally gloomy, equally deprived, equally resigned. Austerity, a word one got very tired of hearing, was presented as something infinitely desirable. The ale I drank in my first English pub was as austere as the most committed socialist could have wished.

Its solitary merit was that it had no taste whatever.

"You know that poem about jolly good ale and old? Is this supposed to be jolly, for God's sweet sake?" Ninette had already been in England for twelve months.

"You get used to it", she said unconvincingly.

"I don't want to get used to it. I'd rather get used to ipecacuanha. Do you suppose they pump this muck up from a disused coal mine?"

"There aren't any disused coal mines. They're all going full blast. Coal mines are a symbol of the triumph of socialism and the age of the common man."

"I'll tell you what it is. This gleet has been brewed in a nationalized factory according to a recipe excogitated by a senior civil servant in the Ministry of something or other. Let's get the hell out of here."

Later on, much later on, things improved. I was again in England one winter after the socialist misery mongers had been momentarily stripped of their power to annoy. Stingo was back on the market. Stingo? It sounded most improbable. I tried it. Magnificent! It was, the pub-keeper told me, an especially potent ale brewed only in the winter months and designed to keep out the cold. It did that all right. If one added, as I invariably did, a measure of vigorous ginger wine or rum, then after downing a pint or two you could rip off coat and jacket and sweater and roll in the snow and it was as though you were sunbathing on the Queensland coast. How can I be so sure? Because, abetted by a jovial Pole who had been dipping into the same mixture, I once did more or less that. We both did. We didn't actually remove our jackets and sweaters but, on leaving the pub, we disposed ourselves very contentedly in deepish snow on the edge of Green Park. We lay there for half-an-hour and would have happily stayed longer but we were ordered off by a cop, obviously concerned for our health. His solicitude was touching but he needn't have bothered. Neither the Pole nor I even sneezed as a result of the experience.

Stingo notwithstanding, English pubs were a let-down. When I first knew them, the owners were determined to be "characters". The role required them to spend the bulk of the opening hours time bawling dismally jocular insults at the customers. The customers themselves, tweed-jacketed and tawnily moustached, guffawed appreciatively as one heavy-bottomed sally succeeded another. "Haw, haw! You're a character, George, you really are a character." You could see that George agreed.

Thirty years after, I looked back on the tweed-jacketed buffoons and the jocular proprietors with a wistful tenderness which I would once have thought inconceivable. The former had vanished - sent to corrective labour camps, for all I know. In their place were disgruntled Jamaicans with ringletted hair or Cockney louts trying to look like Jamaicans. Behind the counter, the jokers had given way to resentful misanthropes whose idea of a witticism would probably have been to slash the customers with a flick knife.

And the food! I'd long since given up hoping for anything along the lines of the feast laid out in Tom Brown's inn. Sausages and mash or cheese and pickled onions would have done me very well - hearty English pub fare, what! The last time I was in England hearty English pub fare consisted of chop suey or chile con came or ravioli, all wrapped in aluminium foil and all tasting vile beyond expression.

In the period between the austerity years and the multicultural years, however, it was possible with a bit of luck to locate an establishment which you could treat with respect and even affection. For some months I had that bit of luck. It led me to a country inn where I stayed while writing a book. There was a greatly gifted chef who produced delicious stews of game which he himself clandestinely slaughtered. The landlord was a companionable fellow with whom I was soon on Christian-name terms. Throughout the inevitable penury of the war years and the doctrinaire penury imposed during the socialist years, Edgar had contrived to preserve a remarkable cellar. Once he actually produced and invited me to share a bottle of homemade parsnip wine which he assured me was close on sixty years old. I anticipated that it would be innocuous and almost certainly undrinkable. It was neither. There wasn't, thank God, a trace of parsnips in the flavour and the effects were redoubtable. The beer came from a tiny local brewery which was probably breaking all kinds of regulations by producing anything so agreeable. Jolly good ale and old began to mean something to me, after all.

I scribbled away in Edgar's inn. The end result was awful but the chefs skill with rook rifle and saucepans together with the resources of Edgar's cellar consoled me. I could have spent the rest of my life in that inn. I wasn't allowed to. There were only two rooms for guests. One evening Edgar timorously announced (timorously because he knew what my reaction would be) that they'd both been booked months earlier. I would have to leave within the week.

"Come off it, Edgar, what the hell are you talking about?"

"I can't help it, Alister. Have a drink?"

"Not on your life, you treacherous hound. I wouldn't drink with you if I were lost in the Sahara. Throw me out now and I'll never finish that damned book of mine."

"Of course you will. Have a drink."

"I thought we were friends."

"So we are but I've promised both rooms to customers who booked them months ago. I can't go back on it. I've got some pre-war cognac..."

"You can keep your lousy cognac."

This hullaballoo took place in the saloon bar. There was only one other customer present. I'd seen him once or twice when he dropped in for a drink or two in the evening. We'd never done more than exchange a civil greeting. He now spoke to me with that self-deprecatory air which is a peculiarity of the English upper classes and in a staccato style reminiscent of Mr Jingle.

"I say - frightful cheek - butting in like this - quite understand tell me to mind own bloody business - but couldn't help overhearing - gather you're writing a book - don't know anything about books myself - rather think you need a bit of peace and quiet to work, what? If bloody old Edgar here won't keep you on - wife and myself delighted put you up - house just a mile or so away - frightfully uncomfortable of course - probably want to move out tomorrow morning - still wife and myself delighted..."

I left Edgar's admirable inn the same night after accepting a glass of that pre-war cognac in sign of my forgiveness. David's old stone house perched in isolation on a hilltop was the reverse of uncomfortable. His wife accepted with the utmost composure the abrupt intrusion of an unknown Australian. I finished the book there and prepared to leave. No question of it.

"Ridiculous, old boy. You can rough it a bit longer, surely. Enjoy having you here." I went on roughing it very comfortably indeed for several more months.

There were two large barrels in David's stone-flagged kitchen. One of them contained ale, from the same irreproachable brewery which supplied Edgar. The other held rough cider, authentic Herefordshire cider, not the better known but inferior cider from Devon or Somerset.

How does it happen that nobody, as far as I've been able to discover, has ever celebrated the merits of that incomparable beverage? I've found nothing in any of the books on my shelves and all that my own lumbering memory has been able to provide is a scrap from a fatuous American ditty which pays homage to "Ida, sweet as apple cider". I wish I could forget it. Its tautology is exasperating: what else could cider be made from if not apples? Above all, the implication that cider is or should be sweet outrages all my finer feelings. The cider which I drew so often from David's barrel was uncompromisingly dry and devoid, moreover, of any carbonated "fizz". It possessed prepotent qualities. Three tankards of the stuff and you knew much more than Apollo. There was no resisting it. It demanded, telepathically, that you should drop whatever you were doing - reading a book or playing a game of chess with David or his wife - and present yourself in the kitchen, tankard in hand, draw a pint, swallow it, draw another and return with it to the living room. The tradition of the house forbade you to serve anyone else. It was every man for himself. A mystical and personal relationship existed between each individual drinker and that wonder-working cider.

Not that any sane man would drink alcohol for therapeutic reasons, but my edition of the Encyclopaedia Britannica - an ancient one, it's true - has a word on this aspect of cider-drinking and perry-drinking (perry was fair enough in its way, I found, but not to be compared to David's Herefordshire cider - nothing was).

The wholesome properties of cider and perry have been recognised by medical men, who recommend them as pleasant and efficacious remedies in affections of a gouty or rheumatic nature, maladies which, strange to say, these very liquors were once supposed to foster, if not actually to originate. Under a similar false impression the notion is general that hard rough cider is apt to cause diarrhoea, colic and kindred complaints, whereas, as a fact, disorders of this kind are conspicuous by their absence in those parts of the country where rough cider and perry constitute the staple drinks of the working-classes. This is especially the case in Herefordshire, which is said also to be the only county in England where no instance of the occurrence of Asiatic cholera has ever been reported.

Of course, it was heartening to know that David's cider would protect me from Asiatic cholera but, after the first taste, I would have gone on drinking it even if I'd been told that that was how you caught Asiatic cholera.

The same edition of the Encyclopaedia affirms that cider is also produced in France, in Germany and, improbably, in the United States. I can't answer for the United States or Germany but I'll wager a hogshead of anything you like that you won't find it in France - not what I call cider. I've spent years trudging from one remote farm to another in Brittany and Normandy and all I've ever been able to sample was the characterless muck which reminded the song-writer of Ida.

ROUND FIVE

An unsuspected Scottish cousin got in touch with me in a roundabout way I can't recall. He lived just on the right or Scottish side of the River Tweed. He was called Elliot. So was everyone else for miles around. We would stop at a garage for petrol.

"And how are you this morning, Mr Elliot."

"Very well, thank you, Mr Elliot. And how are you?"

"Never better, Mr Elliot. By the way, Mr Elliot was in earlier and said he would like to see you." "Well, we're on our way now to call on Mr Elliot. I'll probably bump into Mr Elliot there."

Things were worse still at the pub. My cousin was a frequent and popular customer. He was greeted with a whole frogs' chorus of "Good morning Mr Elliot" while in acknowldgement he himself was compelled to be, so to speak, a one-man chorus: "Good morning, Mr Elliot ... You're looking well, Mr Elliot ... You're not looking at all well, Mr Elliot ... Have you by any chance seen Mr Elliot, Mr Elliot .. ?"

One needed a drink after these dizzying exchanges. The trouble was that everyone was drinking whisky.

> *Let half-starv'd slaves in warmer skies*
> *See future wines, rich-clust'ring rise;*
> *Their lot auld Scotland ne'er envies,*
> *But, blythe and frisky,*

She eyes her freeborn, martial boys
Tak aff their whisky.

That may have been Burns' s view of the matter. It wasn't mine. Australia produced a vicious concoction that went under the name of whisky. We drank it when there was nothing else but it took some doing. Scotch whisky, the blended variety which was all I knew about, wasn't any more to my taste than the Australian substitute.

'Twas whisky made me pawn my clo'es
An' whisky got me a broken nose,
Oh, whisky drove my mother mad
An' whisky nearly killed my dad ...

None of these disasters befell me from drinking whisky - perhaps I didn't drink enough of it; but what I did drink was as appetizing as a compound of bitter aloes and rancid butter. I choked it down with deep revulsion. In my cousin's pub I vehemently refused whisky amid scenes of universal reprehension. I had a lot to learn, I was told. I did indeed.

The revelation came to me on a later trip to Scotland. A friend and I arrived in Edinburgh. In the old town, steep narrow streets (can they have been stepped, which is how I remember them?) led from one gas-lit close to another. Burke and Hare country! To either side, every hundred yards or so, more steps took one down into poky, smoky pubs. We visited a significant number of them. What ill-intentioned Sassenach, I wonder, propagated the notion that Scots are "dour"? It's a monstrous libel, as I soon found out. There was nothing dour about the drinkers in the grubby places we came on that night. My friend's French accent attracted attention and approval. She earned an extra dose of cordiality: the Scots have never forgotten their ancient alliance with

France. And I was Australian? Well, Australians were apparently welcome, too - at least they weren't English.

***

T.W.H.Crosland, an associate of Lord Alfred Douglas, which is alone enough to damn him, had it in for the Scots. A curmudgeonly fellow; an ignorant one, too, since he was apparently unaware that only the Irish and the Americans spell whisky with an "e".

At the same time it is only fair to say that a drunken Scotchman is not by any means a common spectacle, the reason being that the Scot is so inured to the consumption of whiskey from his youth up, that he can take almost any quantity without becoming drunk about the legs. Drink, however, he must have, and both at home and abroad he makes a point of getting as much of it as his means will allow. In Scotland it is quite general for men and women alike to drink whiskey raw and to take the water afterwards. This is done at every meal, and if you call upon a Scotch household at any hour of the day you will be at once offered a four or five-finger dose of the national drink.

This strikes me as a singular indictment. I'm damned if l can see anything blameworthy about being able to hold your liquor nor about offering one's visitors a glass. As to taking whisky neat and following it with a sip of water, no civilized drinker would dream of any other proceeding. The cantankerous Crosland goes on to complain that Scots consider it an insult to refuse a drink. So it is. Annette and I wouldn't have dreamed of refusing the amiable invitations of the customers in those murky Edinburgh pot-houses. It's true that, as in my cousin's pub, some consternation was aroused by our rejection of whisky; but even that was overlooked. Sooner or later, we were assured, we'd realise how mistaken we were. We did.

We became particularly chummy with one member of the company, a jovial kilt-maker called Gordon. What was our programme in Scotland, he wanted to know. Well, Glamis Castle was high on our list. The only authentic fool's motley in existence was to be seen at Glamis. Other people could tour Holyrood Castle if they wanted to. Me, I couldn't wait to see that motley.

Glamis was it? Well, now, that was a most extraordinary coincidence. Gordon was driving right past the castle the very next day. If we liked, he would drop us off there, we could spend a few hours gaping at the fool's motley and maybe looking for some of the innumerable ghosts and the famous secret room and he would pick us up on his way back.

Things began well enough. Gordon deposited us at the castle, promising to collect us in three hours' time, and I started slavering at the prospect of seeing that motley. We were out of luck. The castle was an impressive sight seen from a distance, and from a distance was the only way we saw it. The gates were uncompromisingly shut. No visitors admitted that day. No motley for me.

We were even more out of luck than we at first understood. It was winter, a Scottish winter, with six or eight inches of snow on the ground and a wind decidedly unkinder than man's ingratitude. It didn't merely blow, it subjected you to a protracted Death of the Thousand Cuts. Apart from a tiny village just up against the wall surrounding the Glamis park there was nothing but a polar expanse from horizon to horizon. We made for the pub. It was as firmly closed as the castle gates. That left a little general store and an estate agent's office as the only places of interest. The cold was becoming undendurable. In the store we examined packets of oatmeal for twenty minutes or so. When our absorption in oatmeal had lasted as long as we thought permissible, we bought a few packets and left.

Half an hour slogging through the frozen landscape was all we could stand. The estate agent's office offered a refuge. Until the woman behind the counter began to look openly sceptical we asked about manors and dower houses which would perhaps suit us. We even hinted that we might be interested in Glamis itself. Then we returned to the steppes. It was getting dark. We were, it suddenly occurred to me, on the same latitude as Saint Petersbourg. I didn't see any wolves but I was ready to bet they were lurking nearby, waiting for their opportunity.

It was getting colder. Annette took a purler as we crossed the glacier and hurt her ankle. I didn't give a damn. All I cared about was my own suffering. To hell with Annette and Gordon and Glamis and the fool's motley and Scotland and any wolves in the neighbourhood... This time we concentrated on sardines. It took us another twenty minutes to decide on the particular tin we wanted, then out into the darkness again.

The woman in the estate agent's office looked as though she might call the police at any moment. Our inquiries about freeholds and fishing rights got no more than a grunt from her. We met with the same suspicion when we returned to the general store for the third time. Apart from the sardines and oatmeal there wasn't anything much on the shelves but the proprietoress had obviously begun to think we were casing the joint.

"Isn't there anywhere where we could find some shelter?"

"We could try to build an igloo."

"Do go on being entertaining. It's such a comfort. I think I'll just lie down and freeze to death. I can't stand this another minute. Mon Dieu, what wouldn't I give to be back in Paris! I'm dying, I tell you! Fool's motley! I'm the one who ought to be wearing fool's motley. I must have been crazy to let you drag me into this."

"It's not my fault. How was I to know we were taking on something that would have scared the hell out of Amundsen?"

Both of us felt like crying. As a matter of fact, I think I'd actually begun to cry when suddenly... I saw... the Aurora Borealis? A snow mirage? Hallucination preceding death from freezing? By God! It was a lighted window! The pub was open!

I've met some very pleasant landlords in my time but never one to whom I took such an instantaneous liking.

"Ye're looking a wee bit chilled."

If anyone else had made that particular remark at that particular moment I would have killed him. As it was, I gave him a great big smile. I think I even added that there was a bit of a nip in the air.

"Well, sit you down by the fire and I'll give you something to wann ye up."

We were too far gone for the fire to do us much good but one gulp from the glasses served to us and I knew we were going to be all right. What was it, this astonishing potion? The landlord was fairly flabbergasted. Didn't I know? It was a single malt whisky, a ten-year-old Talisker from the island of Skye. So this was what was meant by whisky! To think that I'd been snootily refusing it all these years! And to think that the unspeakable Crosland wanted to mix this miraculous liquid with water! No wonder he'd been a crony of Lord Alfred Douglas.

Malt whisky became a religion to me from that first sip. Before long I had become so ritualistic that I refused to drink it from a glass. Only a quaich would do, the traditional shallow two-handled bowl. I spent a long time before I found one that suited me. It was a marvel, not much bigger than an egg-cup and formed of wooden staves bound round with osier. Within a month or two my small son had taken it apart and thirty odd years later I have still not quite forgiven him.

That Talisker transformed me into a sort of counterfeit Scot. It actually impelled me to learn Gaelic. Or to try and learn it. The language's irregular verbs and verbal nouns put an end to that particular fantasy. It wasn't altogether a wasted effort though. Instead of disgracing myself by mumbling, "Here's luck" or something equally uncouth when some Gaelic-speaking drinker wishes me "Good health" - Slainte mhath - I can come back forthrightly with Slainte mhor - "Great health".

Over the years since that consummate evening in the pub at Glamis I've drunk innumerable single malts, on one occasion a fifty-year-old Macallan, one dram of which cost me all I had to live on for the rest of the week. On another occasion I acquired - from my friend Pascal, a wine-grower friend in the middle of France, of all improbable benefactors - a bottle of the rarest of all single malts, the fabulous Ardbeg. I drank every drop of it myself, never for a moment considering the possibility of offering so much as a taste to anyone else. Each malt that's come my way - Bunnahabhain, Glenmorangie, Glenlivet, Ohan, Lagavulin - declared itself of the same family and yet the variations between them were as numerous and as subtle as between wines. I loved them all - perhaps sentimentally preserving a secret place among my taste buds for the revelatory Talisker.

ROUND SIX

Really, there is a fortune waiting for the first man who starts a calvados trade in England. It is one of the purest and most potent drinks in existence. One can get blind in 10 minutes, unfailingly-yet it's not even imported to England - and it could be made by the gallon *in ea parte quae dicitur Westcuntre'*, being but the spirit of that staple product cider.

Now how could any respectable young man fail to respond to that juicy passage in a letter of Peter Warlock's? Not I. From the moment I first read it in Cecil Gray's biography of Warlock, I fairly slavered at the thought of calvados. But it was no more readily available in Australia than it had been in Warlock's England. For that very reason, it became an obsession with me, just like that jolly good ale and old. When other people thought of France they thought of the Louvre or Napoleon's tomb or the Eiffel Tower. I thought of calvados.

Right after the war, which was when I finally made it to France, everything was in short supply. The only aperitif readily available was evidently compounded of eye of newt and toe of frog, wool of bat and tongue of dog, although according to the label it was distilled (and this sounded and was as revolting as any eye of newt) from artichokes. In the restaurants you could only get wine if the proprietor knew you and it was served in cups as in a Prohibition-era speakeasy. You had as much chance of getting cognac at the end of your meal as you would have had at a meeting of the Plymouth Brethren. I'd travelled thirteen thousand miles or whatever it was and it looked as though calvados was as remote as ever.

One should never despair in France. In the very first cafe I entered on my very first evening in Paris, lo! a miracle took place. I expected my hesitant inquiry about calvados to be submerged in derision. Far from it. The patron was a Nonnan. Not only did he have calvados, it was calvados of his own making. "Just try that, *vous m'en direz des nouvelles.*" I tried it. I looked up at the patron with what the stylists would call a beatific smile. The patron smiled back and his smile was pretty beatific, too. I didn't have to say anything. He understood. He poured me another.

Either Warlock had less of a head for alcohol than I did or he managed to drink a hell of a lot more calvados in ten minutes than I could manage. I was still comparatively sober after my fourth (or was it fifth?) glass. But it was everything I'd hoped for as to flavour - apples on a spree - and in due course I was able to confirm that Warlock had not exaggerated its potency.

I adopted the proletarian habit of drinking a glass with my morning coffee - a far better beginning to the day than bacon and eggs. The French may not produce cider comparable to the inspiriting cider of Hertfordshire; but there's no denying that they know what to do with such cider as they do produce.

What lay ahead, although I didn't know it, was something still more astonishing than calvados.

***

Absinthe, je t' adore, certes!
Il me semble, quandje te bois,
Humer l'ame desjeunes bois,
Pendant la belle saison verte!

Raoul Ponchon had the right outlook, no question of that. But I'd always had a deep conviction that if I could only get hold of a bottle of absinthe myself I'd write poetry much better than his. For that matter, I thought there was a fair chance that a diet of absinthe would at once ensure that I wrote better poetry than Verlaine's or Rimbaud's or Baudelaire's (notable absinthe drinkers, all of them) and while I was at it painted pictures which were right up there with those of Lautrec or Gauguin or Van Gogh, likewise devotees of the green fairy, as absinthe was known to its adepts. By dint of reading about it I'd come to believe that absinthe possessed talismanic properties. It was as high on my list of priorities as calvados.

I should have known. Like every other country, France has always had its fair share of wowsers and omniscient medicos (a certain Dr Magnan in particular played an ignoble role in connexion with absinthe) and meddlesome politicians and every other variety of pestilential evangelist. The sight of so many people getting so much enjoyment out of absinthe was more than this riff-raff could stand. Through their joint efforts (with a bit of help from that damned ola and his Assommoir) absinthe was prohibited on the black 16th of March 1915. As far as I could see I was never going to taste absinthe and my poetry would be what it always had been.

But a few of the great French distilleries, I learnt, continued to produce absinthe in Spain. In my local cafe I was on friendly terms with a truck-driver. His route? Valencia-Paris, once a week. And I had no trouble persuading him to undertake a little genteel smuggling. By the time we brought our operation to an end I'd acquired close on one hundred bottles. I gave one or two sips to a few favoured friends. For the rest, with a single exception which I'll get around to explaining, I was no more generous with my absinthe than I'd been with my Ardbeg.

I had acted just in time. Because, of course, the busybodies were lying in wait. As soon as Spain got itself enmeshed in the lugubrious "European Community", the supra-bureaucrats of Brussels demanded as proof of submission that Spain in turn abandon its unholy role as a purveyor of absinthe.

Meantime, it was everything I'd imagined, the green fairy. I didn't manage to clobber Baudelaire and the rest of them but that didn't even matter anymore. The very colour of absinthe was intoxicating, mesmeric, you could stare at your glass for hours and gradually enter into a trance-like state without even putting your lips to it. "A glass of absinthe", Oscar Wilde announced, "is as poetical as anything in the world. What difference is there between a glass of absinthe and a sunset?" Plenty, is the answer to that one. Nothing could be less like absinthe than a sunset unless there's such a thing as a green sunset. And if there were, it couldn't possibly be the same green, a bewitching, a unique, a magical green, a green that nature has never matched.

Wilde didn't give his opinion as to the taste of absinthe. If his inept comment on the colour is anything to go by, that's probably just as well. Innumerable imbeciles over the years have compared it to aniseed. Can they ever have tasted it? Would anyone but an imbecile attempt to compare it to the flavour of any other substance on earth? The taste of absinthe is as strange, as spellbinding, as otherworldly as its colour.

A further touch of necromancy was introduced, I discovered, when it came to preparing what, for once in a way, may fairly be described as the elixir. When so engaged, I always had a feeling that I ought to be wearing a star-spangled conical hat and standing inside a pentagram. Because it was a ceremonious business. Absinthe was not something to be vulgarly guzzled, it was consumed ritually, with reverence. The precise amount had to be decanted (too much coarsened the flavour), a pierced spoon (known as a "pelle" or spade) was laid across the glass, a lump of sugar was placed on the spoon and through this water was allowed to percolate, drop by drop. Paracelsus would have felt right at home preparing absinthe.

There was nothing to stop you using a jug or a carafe from which to pour the water; but pre-1916 every cafe had a "fountain" on the bar - a glass bowl filled with ice water and perched on a pewter column. It was equipped with four tiny spigots. You opened one of these and allowed the water to fall slowly onto the sugar. At a certain moment the mixture would cloud, retaining however its original mysterious colour instead of assuming the turgid khaki hue which characterizes "pastis", the unworthy successor to absinthe.

With a hundred bottles to be drunk, I badly wanted a fountain, I almost felt I was entitled to one. But none had been manufactured for thirty years or more. The patron of my local cafe when I applied to him was not optimistic. His own fountain, or rather his father's had been thrown out or lost long ago. He seemed to remember, though, that the aged bootmaker a few doors down had been a great absinthe drinker in his day. Perhaps he could help.

No, the bootmaker no longer had a fountain, either. But the shop where he had bought one in his youth still existed. Just possibly ...

The shop in question specialized in cafe supplies and the moment I entered it I felt a surge of hope. It was dusty and disordered and looked as though nothing had changed there since the building first went up - in 1895, according to the date inscribed on the facade. The shop-keeper himself looked as though he'd been around for considerably longer.

"I don't suppose you'd have an absinthe fountain by any chance?"

"An absinthe fountain! Now where on earth did a young fellow like you ever hear about absinthe fountains?"

"I can't remember who told me but I must have one. I've got the absinthe already."

"You've got absinthe! You mean real absinthe, not some filthy homemade pastis?"

"Real absinthe."

"You wait there."

He vanished into the back room. There was a sound as of crates and things being moved around. Finally, the antique proprietor reappeared with a couple of dilapidated packages.

"Absinthe fountains, two of them!" He looked at the heiroglyphs on the wrapping. "They've been here - would you believe it? - for nearly sixty years. My poor old father ... "

"I suppose you wouldn't consider selling them? Or even one of them?"

The old boy looked me over.

"You say you've got some absinthe?"

"Yes, I have."

"Real absinthe?"

"Real absinthe."

"I'll tell you what. You come back tomorrow and I'll let you know if I'm prepared to sell you these fountains. Tomorrow, d'accord?"

I thought I knew what was expected of me. When I came back the next day I brought a bottle of my absinthe with me. My guess had been right. One of the fountains had already been taken out of its packaging and was standing on the counter. A couple of glasses and two pelles and a bowl of sugar were beside it.

"I thought you might like a glass of absinthe, Monsieur. I've got some here."

"Real absinthe?"

"Real absinthe."

We prepared two glasses ritually. We sipped sacramentally. We had another. And a third for luck.

"You'll allow me to leave the rest of the bottle with you?"

"And you'll allow me to give you one of my fountains. Believe me, I'm getting the better of the bargain. Real absinthe!"

His generosity deserved more than a half-empty bottle. Next day I gave him a full one. At that point, I think he would have let me help myself to the entire contents of his shop.

Absinthe! Despite a minimum alcoholic content of 68 - against a derisory 40 or so for such beverages as vodka - absinthe is not, strictly speaking, a drunkard's drink. As a matter of fact there is something distasteful about describing it as a drink at all. It induces no desire to brawl or blubber or guffaw or reel or retch. It produces an ineffable quietude which Arthur Symons evoked to perfection in his sonnet, "The Absinthe-Drinker".

Gently I wave the visible world away.
Far off, I hear a oar, afar yet near,
Far off and strange, a voice is in my ear,
And is the voice my own? the words I say
Fall strangely, like a dream, across the day;
And the dim sunshine is a dream. How clear,
New as the world to lovers' eyes, appear
The men and women passing on their way!

The world is very fair. The hours are all
Linked in a dance of mere forgetfulness.
I am at peace with God and man. O glide,
Sands of the hour-glass that I count not, fall
Serenely: scarce I feel your soft caress,
Rocked on this dreamy and indifferent tide.

You can take it from me that drinking absinthe to achieve this state of quasi-mystical ecstasy is a good deal more enjoyable than reciting "Om" fifty thousand times to obtain the same effect.

***

Not all doctors have shown themselves as reprehensible as the odious Magnan. Leon Daudet is my idea of the right sort of doctor. He never practiced (it would have been better for the population ifhe had) but he did complete a medical course with some distinction and his diagnoses must therefore betaken seriously. It's true that he, too, had a censorious attitude towards absinthe (he disapproved of all aperitifs) but it was nothing like as censorious as his attitude towards water.

I have always been persuaded that the vast majority of depressive, debilitated and neurasthenic individuals who in pre-war days dragged themselves lethargically from one consulting-room to another owed their condition to an over-indulgence in tap water and mineral waters.

His own prescription for preserving mental and physical health was to drink wine in almost as impressive quantities as Squire Mytton: he recorded his consumption as three bottles a day (not including a pint of champagne by way of a mild stimulant before dinner) but friends of his have assured me that he could always be persuaded to increase the dose.

Most of Daudet's contemporaries would have agreed with his view that wine was simultaneously a source of pleasure unlike any other, an irreplaceable contribution to harmony among individuals and a vital element of diet.

A later generation would unhappily have been less enthusiastic. Things had changed by the time I reached France. The old reverential attitude towards wine had been vitiated by the fact that during the war it had rarely been possible to get hold of anything worth drinking (stamped across the label of the first bottle of champagne I saw in France were the words - in German - "Reserved for Officers of the Wehrmacht"). Older people returned to wine with a sob of relief. On the other hand, in the years immediately after the war, something even more obnoxious than tap water was introduced by the American troops - revolting carbonated "soft drinks" with offensive brand names and still more offensive flavours which were ingurgitated with apparent enjoyment by young people who, in pre-war days, would have been able to distinguish a first from a second growth by the time they were five.

ROUND SEVEN

Maurice Chevalier used to sing a little song about the Quai de Bercy.

Quai de Bercy, quai de la cloche,
Sous Jes tonneaux de pinard,
Sans un radis, rien clans la poche,
On respire le pommard.

The Quai de Bercy was the distribution centre for wine in Paris. The alleys were lined with warehouses and, as Chevalier's song put it, you inhaled the fumes of pommard as you walked past them, along with those of chateauneuf-du-pape, chinon, cahors, muscadet and virtually any other wine you care to mention. It wasn't necessary to content oneself with these delicious whiffs, either. The warehouse masters were a genial lot and if, after chatting with you for a while, they decided you were the right sort, they would give you the freedom of their barrels.

On the left bank was the wine market, the Hailes aux Vins. This was another conglomeration of warehouses and cellars grouped around alleys with noble names - the rue de Graves, the rue de Champagne, the rue de Bordeaux.

Your reception here, so long as you displayed a proper deference and eagerness for instruction, was just as cordial as on the Quai de Bercy. I spent some unforgettable hours in both places.

It was only to be expected, I suppose. Politicians and town-planners, the most horrible coalition ever to come into existence, saw the Quai de Bercy and the Halle aux Vins as their natural prey. The former has long since been razed to make way for an inconceivably hideous sports stadium. No doubt the town-planners got an extra fillip from reflecting that athletes are notorious water-drinkers.

As to the Halle aux Vins, that has been given over in part to a university building where scowling adolescents are too busy clamoring for special consideration to enjoy drinking wine. And in part to a Centre for Islamic Studies with the koranic prohibition of alcohol doubtless figuring largely in the curriculum. I wouldn't put it past the planners and politicians to have had that in mind from the beginning. How the brutes must have relished tearing down the Halle aux Vins in order to lodge fanatical teetotalers.**

That was an extraordinary period, so soon after the war. No-one was actually dancing in the streets, the manifestations of jubilation had ceased. But there was an astonishing sense of confidence which made everyone relaxed and ready to enjoy things. There has never been quite the same outgoing spirit since. Even if they still existed, I doubt if the Quai de Bercy and the Hailes aux Vins would extend so warm a welcome to strangers - foreign strangers, at that - as they did in those buoyant post-war days. I don't suppose, either, that I would meet with the same reception as we encountered, an Australian friend and myself, when we decided that a trip to Chablis was imperative.

Which café, we wondered when we got there, would be the best place to start our investigation? We stopped a passer-by in the street and asked him. Where, he wanted to know, had we come from? Australia? He'd never expected to meet Australians, *Ça va, non.* We cunningly hinted - I think we actually asserted - that we had left Australia expressly in order to drink chablis. It was the right move. Gesturing towards a hillside, "You see over there?" this friendly fellow asked. "The five best vine-yards of Chablis are on that slope. I own three of them. Come with me". We went with him.

It was the first time I'd been in a French wine-grower's cellar - it must have been the first time I'd been in a cellar of any kind. The vaulted stone roof, the musty smell, the cobwebs, the recumbent bottles - I loved them all, instantaneously and for ever. Except when, to our astonishment, we were invited to lunch in the huge kitchen, we spent most of the day in the cellar, savouring wines that I will certainly never taste again. After a while I began to calculate uneasily how much this was all going to cost. I needn't have worried. It wasn't going to cost anything. This was no vulgar commercial transaction; against all reason, it was made clear that we were guests of the house.***

Three generations ruled the vineyards to which we were given access. The grandfather was the happiest of the three. For fifty years or so, he had lived a life of self-abnegation. An untainted palate was essential for the proper appraisal of each year's vintage. That meant that he could not drink, merely roll the wine around in his mouth, meditate on it and then - I could imagine his anguish he did so - spit it out. To smoke a single cigarette would have made him a hissing and a by-word throughout the district. Now his son had reached an age where he could be trusted to take over. There was a grandson, too, who had foregone the same pleasures and who was equipped to step in in an emergency. At long last, the patriarch could actually swallow the sublime product of his labour. He could even fulfil) a lifetime's ambition and smoke a pipe.

***

Some years later I called again on that noble family. Only the grandson was at home. "You won't remember me . . . "

"Of course I do. You came here with another Australian."

"What a memory! How's your father?"

"He's very well. He's out in the vineyards but he'll be back soon."

"And your grandfather?"

"Dead."

"I'm sorry to hear that." I was, too.

"You needn't be. It was last winter. He was sitting by the fire with a glass of wine beside him and his pipe in his hand. When we went to tell him it was bedtime - he was dead. You couldn't want a better death than that."

It sounds, I'm aware, like a sentimental novelist's invention. But I'm no novelist and not conspicuously sentimental. That's how it was.

***

Drinking in Paris cafes was second only to drinking in a cellar. They are disappearing at a fearsome rate. I've forgotten how many vanish every year-quite a few hundreds, at any rate. Most of those that survive have bedecked themselves with jukeboxes and pinball machines, plastic furniture and neon lights. You can order a lemonade or a ginger ale or a glass of milk and no one will give you a dirty look.

The ones I knew were very different. Smoking had not yet been proclaimed a manifestation of the Diabolic Principle and you had to grope through a sort of smog compounded of the fumes from Gauloises and Gitanes and Voltigeurs and, for the really impoverished, Elégantes which were about as elegant as Hairy Ainus but which could be bought individually for a few centimes. Plastic had no place in these cafes of mine. The tables had marble tops on which dice and dominoes made an agreeable clunk. If a jukebox had been introduced it would have been overturned and its innards wrenched out by the customers.

You would have had to be downright foolhardy to order milk or lemonade in these places. When things got back to normal after the war you could order practically anything else. I worked steadily through the whole range, coming on what, to me, were unknown and delectable drinks. In winter I favoured a resin-based aperitif which when mixed with hot water protected you against the worst that Paris could do in the way of cold. In summer, I switched to a concoction made from gentian root. It was supposed to be the preferred drink of alcoholics since its extreme bitterness made it the only thing they could taste. I drank it because I liked it.

Mostly, though, since I was none too rich at the time, I drank ordinary red wine, gros rouge. Even I could tell that it was not up to Jimmy Watson's standards. It was genuine rotgut as a rule but the mere fact of drinking it in a Paris cafe somehow made it palatable.

ROUND EIGHT

Not long after I arrived in France I was staying with Richard Aldington, a writer I had admired since my schooldays, at his villa on the Mediterranean coast. In the train on my way South I thought of a a passage in his memoirs and felt slightly apprehensive:

... a man should not drink after forty - wine is for the young. I scouted this as a paradox when it was first told me, but having passed the fatal date line I am inclined to think it embodies a truth. Except in the Naples bust, Bacchus is always represented as a young man. How right those artists were in their intuitions!

Did this mean that my encounter with a man I so greatly esteemed was to be celebrated with cups of tea? I needn't have worried. Five minutes after I turned up, I was seated with Richard and his wife with a bottle before us.

Richard was no pedant in the matter of wine. Nobody could have loved the great burgundies and bordeaux more than he did but he could be content with obscure and unremarkable vintages as long as they were essentially sound. The trouble was that, with the war only just ended, good wine of any sort was in short supply. We drank whatever we could get and what we got was usually pretty awful, I now realise. Richard grimaced with every mouthful. I thought it was delicious.

I couldn't convince Richard that my enjoyment, however misplaced, was nonetheless genuine. He attributed my happy guzzling to mere politeness.

"Civility is out of place when it comes to wine, my dear fellow. Lie as much as you like about everything else but wine deserves the truth. And the truth about this nauseating liquid I've been giving you is that it would doubtless do a good job of unclogging bathroom pipes but that it - is - bloody - well - undrinkable!"

"I'm sorry, Richard, but I like it."

With a commiserating nod as though I'd agreed with every word of his denunciation, "Never mind, never mind. France has a miraculous resilience. You'll see, one of these days you'll find out what wine really is. "

I found out much sooner than I could have hoped. There was an excellent restaurant in the nearby village.

Richard had known the proprietor from pre-war days. Whenever we went there the two of them would join together in a sort of graveside requiem.

"How long are we going to have to wait before we can get something worth drin king, Monsieur Jean?"

"Ah, Monsieur Aldington, if only I could tell you! When I think of some of the wines I used to serve you before the war ... "

"I think of them, too, Monsieur Jean, believe me!"

And, as though lamenting the death of a much-loved relation, " I always remember that Gruaud-Larose- Lascases of 1923 ... "

"The 1918 Haut-Brion ... "

"The 1904 Chateau-Lafite ... "

These lachrymose exchanges must have continued for a good six months or more. I think both Richard and Monsieur Jean rather missed them when they came to an end. They had to come to an end, however. That "miraculous resilence" of France to which Richard had alluded proved to be a reality. Entering the restaurant one evening we were approached by Monsieur Jean in a singularly exalted state.

"Monsieur Aldington", he said with a distinct catch in his voice, "tonight, at long last, tonight I can offer you a true wine. "

It was a La Tache, although to my shame, I no longer recall the year, and I drank it, as Richard had prophesied, with a sense of wonder, almost of incredulity. So this was what he had been talking about!

It was my first meeting with a truly great wine.

I don't know how much Richard had to pay for this marvel - the equivalent, I would guess, of 500. From time to time, reminiscing with the tiresome wistfulness of the aged, I've mentioned that astonishing occasion and, on being asked, have put the price at some such figure. The reaction of a handful of boobies has been one of moral outrage. Never - not even if they were millionaires - would they pay such a sum for a mere bottle of wine. For a set of golf clubs, for a new suit, for two weeks floundering about at a ski resort, for a down payment on a life insurance policy - by all means; but for a bottle of wine, no. It simply wouldn't be worth it.

Well, it's now, God help me, some fifty years since I helped empty that bottle of La Tache and I can still recall the taste, the colour, the aroma with almost as much enjoyment as when I was actually drinking it. A pleasure which lasts for fifty years strikes me as cheap at any price.

***

That bottle of La Tache signalled a return to better times, in fact to the best times. Among other things champagne - what I had hitherto known as "fizzy wine" - came to figure as an essential element in our diet. For some reason, the sort of people who give the impression that drinking is a melancholy duty rather than a pleasure won't have anything to do with champagne. It isn't, they mysteriously affirm, really a wine at all. Me, I can' t get enough of it. Or at any rate I only did so once. That was when a group of high-minded friends gave me for my birthday a Nebuchadnezzar of it - a towering vessel containing the equivalent of twenty bottles. My recollection is that it stood about two metres high. That may be a memory slightly distorted by the fact that we emptied it in the course of an evening between five of us. What I do clearly recall is that I had to fill the bath with blocks of ice in order to chill it.

If they hadn't been such rarities as to be almost unprocurable, I don't doubt that Richard would have happily provided a nebuchadnezzar for our morning aperitif. As it was, he and his wife and I made do with a simple magnum each day before lunch and another before dinner - without prejudice, as the lawyers say, to whatever we might drink with the meal. Sometimes this would be more champagne. Germans (or so Richard claimed) were in the habit of drinking champagne throughout the meal -" and a very good habit, too", he would assure us, "so long as it's carried to excess." From time to time, then, he would propose, "Let's be Boches this evening." I had no objection.

I don't recall ever seeing Richard drunk although he could put down awe-inspiring quantities of wine. Remembering one particular evening, I raise my glass to his memory. Half a dozen friends of his were staying at the villa. Two friends of my own, Geoffrey Dutton and the Hibernian Deasey, had installed themselves at the local inn and had been invited to dinner.

At the end of the meal, Richard followed his usual practice and opened a magnum of champagne. The women helped us to empty it and then disappeared to their bedrooms. Richard opened another magnum and another. A couple of the guests looked a bit dilapidated by the time we' d finished these and went off to bed with their wives. That left Richard with his two remaining guests and Deasey and Dutton and me. Richard opened another magnum. It was enough to send his two friends scampering out of harm's way. Deasey and Dutton and I remained to uphold the honour of Australia or possibly, in Deasey's case, of Ireland.

We didn't uphold it for long. Another glass or two and Dutton tottered wamblingly back to his inn. Simultaneously, I went off to bed, too, and spent a few hideous hours watching the room revolve on its own axis.

Next morning I visited the inn to see how Dutton and Deasey were feeling. I hoped they were feeling as unhappy as I was. They were. None of us said anything for ten minutes or so. There didn't seem anything to say. Finally, "How much longer did you hold out?" I asked Deasey.

"For about as long as Black Monro - may the pit be hot for him! - held out against The O'Neill. After you two had scuttled like a pair of misbegotten Black-and-Tans, Richard opened another magnum. Well, for all that me belly was protesting to a fearsome degree, I helped him drink it. Then I knew me time had come and I just managed to get outside where1 brought up everything I'd eaten and drunk all day. And d'ye know what?

Just before darkness fell on me, I looked around and that bloody Richard, all by himself, was opening another magnum! I tell you, if I'd had me strength I would've gone back inside and killed the murderin' spalpeen!"

Bismarck, I read somewhere or other, could put a bottle of champagne to his lips and empty it without drawing breath. Richard, although he would have deplored such behaviour, could unquestionably have managed the same feat if he had had a mind to.

***

Not everyone who came to the villa shared Richard's (and my) enthusiasm for champagne. The South African poet Roy Campbell was staying with his family not far away and would drop in most days. He drank his wine from tumblers filled to the brim.

A heeltap! a heeltap! I never could bear it!

So fill me a bumper, a bumper of claret!

Let the bottle pass freely, don 't shirk it nor spare it,

For a heeltap! a heeltap! I never could bear it!

Those were exactly Roy's sentiments. Except that his bumpers weren't filled with claret, let alone champagne. Waving aside the finest offerings from Richard' s cellar, he called clamorously for the raw red wine of dubious origin which was kept expressly for him. Even before Richard had undertaken my oenological education, I doubt if I could have swallowed it. Roy would toss down a pint of his intimidating plonk in a single sustained gulp. It was something to see.

When he wasn't swigging his gros rouge with Richard he liked nothing more than to consume it in one of the local cafes where the fishermen gathered after unloading their catch. They thought highly of Roy, not only because he was the best company in the world with an inexhaustible repertoire of astonishing yams but because, through the bush telegraph, they knew that in his time he had been a professional fisherman himself further down the coast. They also knew that he had been something of a star in the Provencal bullfights and in the famous water jousts which took place each year. But what impressed them even more than this heroic past was that gargantual swallow of his which had awed Richard and me. They were awe-inspiring drinkers themselves but none of them was a match for Roy.

Only once did I see him on the verge of defeat and then for no more than a few seconds. He had just gulped down his seventh or eighth tumbler when suddenly his face was contorted and large beads of sweat broke out on his forehead. His lips were clamped tightly shut but his throat muscles worked convulsively. For a moment, I was afraid he'd had some sort of attack. But no. His features returned to normal, he straightened up and indicated with a gesture to the cafe proprietor that he wanted another glass. Turning to me, " I'm sorry about that, man", he rumbled in his thick Natal accent, "but I just vomited."

***

Coming from Australia, I could never get used to the idea that it was possible to move from one country to another in an hour or so. It finally occurred to me that Italy was no distance from where Richard had his villa and it seemed sound commonsense to go and investigate Italian wine on the spot.

So far my knowledge of Italian wines had been limited to the inconceivably nauseating mixture of cochineal and surgical spirit which was served in Melbourne's less expensive restaurants. It cost sixpence a half litre, if I remember correctly, and was grossly overpriced at that. Roy would have loved it. I wasn't, then, expecting to come on anything in the La Tache class and I didn't. But I didn't do too badly either. There were occasional unpleasant incidents (Asti Spumante was one of them) but the good encounters far outnumbered the unpleasant ones. I started in Rome and then headed for Florence, conscientiously sipping all the way. Obviously, if one was going to drink anything at all in Florence (and I was) it had to be Chianti. I did my best to work through the 7 million gallons of Chianti Classico which the district produces each year and decided that it would meet Richard's severe standards. A captivating wine. Stimulating, too. Over stimulating, perhaps, because after drinking rather more than my usual allowance one day, I suddenly had the insane notion of walking from Florence to Bologna. If only it had remained a notion! But no; the Chianti urging me on, I actually started out. By nightfall the Chianti had let me down. I'd had enough - of walking, that is. As far as I was concerned, the rest of the jaunt (I don't suppose I'd covered more than about 15 kilometres) would be by train or bus or, if these weren't available, by chauffeur-driven limousine or chartered plane, by ox cart, on horseback. From now on, you wouldn't catch me walking any further than the nearest bar.

Apart from anything else I was thirsty - I usually was in those days - and it was more or less with a sob of relief that I espied an inn isolated on the lonely road. I might have resolved never to walk again but that inn had me running towards it. The benevolent-looking proprietor (the men whose business it is to slake thirsts are invariably benevolent-looking, I've noticed) asked me what I wanted. At least I suppose that was what he asked: I didn't know any Italian. Remembering films in which parched travellers had coped with the same problem when coming on compassionate natives, I threw my head back, opened my mouth in an idiot gape and pointed to it with anguished finger.

The good man disappeared briefly and returned with an unlabelled bottle containing, I felt sure, wine of some sort. I drank the whole lot in four or five life-saving gulps. Delicious! You didn' t have to be as thirsty as I was to rejoice in it.

"That' s good wine of yours, " I told the inn-keeper. Let me have another bottle , will you?" That was the sense of my remark but what I actually said was, "Il tuoi vino e motto buon o, Commendatore, vorrei un ' altra bottiglia, per favore." As I hope to be saved, that's what I said and with a pronounced Tuscan accent that would have had you gasping. Ten minutes earlier, if l'd been asked whether I spoke Italian, I would have replied truthfully that I didn't, not a word. Now here I was, chattering away as though it were my mother tongue. What's more, I wasn't in the least surprised, it seemed the most natural thing in the world.

By the time I'd finished the second bottle, I was able to invite the inn-keeper to join me in a third, employing a number of highly idiomatic phrases which no ordinary foreigner would have known. The third bottle was conclusive. Half way through it I started putting the inn-keeper right about his use of the subjunctive. I lost count of the number of bottles we downed between the two of us. I know that before I groped my way to bed I was quoting freely from Petrarch and Dante and Ariosto together with a number of almost forgotten 13th-century lyric poets. I also invented a few tales in the manner of Boccacio and I don't mind saying that there was simply no comparison between my style and his. The inn-keeper was addressing me as Dottore and I don't blame him.

Trebianno, that's what I'd been drinking, but it's no good ordering it and expecting to achieve the same mastery of the Italian language as I acquired. Because Trebbiano, it was eventually explained to me, was not the name of a specific wine but of a grape variety. Experience forced me to realise that not all wines made from the Trebbiano grape possess the same linguistic gifts as the one I drank that night.

My Trebbiano was not merely a unique language teacher. It was also, unlike most of the teachers I've had to do with, altogether opposed to the infliction of punishment. This was clear next morning when, in spite of all I'd drunk, I woke up feeling wonderfully well. Still, I thought a cup of coffee would be agreeable . Downstairs, I opened my mouth to give my order. It stayed open. Not one word of my bountiful Italian vocabulary remained. I threw back my head, opened my mouth a bit wider and pointed to it.

ROUND NINE

Not long afterwards I decided to settle definitively in Paris where I wouldn't need any wizard's wine to enable me to converse with the locals. There was no shortage of drinking companions. The sort of Frenchmen I mostly associated with - taxi-drivers and plumbers and shop-keepers - liked nothing better than to spend an hour or two at the end of the day consuming more wine or pastis than wowserdom would approve. The two men who became my regular associates in debauchery, however, were not French. They were Russians, Soviet Russians, and I was to watch, unbelievingly, while they outdid Deasey or Roy or anyone else I'd ever encountered.

When I first saw them they were playing chess in a cafe I used to frequent. That was against all the rules. You played dice in Paris cafes or a (to me) incomprehensible card game called belote. If sufficiently elderly you were allowed to play dominoes . What nobody in the history of that cafe had ever played before was chess. The Russians' eccentric pastime had attracted a small group of baffled onlookers.

I was a chess player myself - sort of. Any reasonably intelligent five-year-old could checkmate me in six moves but at least I knew enough to be impressed by the Russians' skill. When the game was over I told them that, as a result of studying their expert performance, I hoped that in future it might take my opponent seven or perhaps eight moves to checkmate me.

"Glad to have been of assistance. Have a drink."

I couldn't say how many times I was to hear the last three words in the years ahead..

The Russians were drinking whisky without any visible relish. In the interests of Australian-Soviet friendship I ordered vodka for myself. My chess moves might have been clumsy, but on this occasion at any rate, my social move couldn't be faulted. As a basis for friendship with Russians, calling for vodka was the thing to do all right. I think these particular Russians had been conscientiously trying to adapt to Western ways. Now, taking their lead from me, they abandoned the attempt, shoved their whisky aside and ordered vodkas for themselves. All that the cafe could offer was a killjoy concoction distilled somewhere in the outer suburbs of Paris. Igor and Sasha grimaced like Richard trying to swallow a glass of Algerian red.

"This isn't vodka! We can make better vodka in Russia out of potato peelings and old boots. You'd better come with us and we'll give you some vodka worthy of the name."

It was Sasha's flat we went to first. His wife knew what was expected of her. She had a couple of bottles on the table almost before we closed the door behind us. In the time it took Sasha to rip off the foil cap and bring out glasses,' he had added a dish of pickled mushrooms, a dish of sprats and a dish of piroshki. Also, I was impressed to see, a large bowl of caviar. Then the vodka was poured.

I've been hunting for some apposite quotation to lighten up this recital as I've tried to do in preceding chapters. No luck. Vodka seems to have been as neglected by the poets as shamefully as cider. Esenin himself, who by all accounts virtually lived on it, hasn't written a single line about vodka as far as I can see. Perhaps he was so busy drinking the stuff that he had no time to write about it.

Or perhaps he was so overwhelmed by its ineffable seduction that he could find no words in which to convey it. Well, to nobody's surprise I take it, I can't do any better than Esenin. I wish I could. I owe vodka an ode, a sonnet sequence, an anacreontic - a prothalamion even, because if ever there was a marriage to be celebrated it was my union with vodka.

The same dolts who maintain that absinthe tastes of aniseed assert that vodka doesn't taste of anything at all. I remember an American advertisement for it which sought to lure the customers with some such insane slogan as, "For those who like the effect of alcohol but not the taste of alcohol." Incredible! I've never claimed to have a "palate" and I won't say I can readily distinguish a Moskovskaya from a Stolichnayaor a Stolichnaya from a Kubanskaya. What I will claim - and anyone who wants to put me to the test, at his or her expense, will be heartily welcome - is that I can instantaneously recognise the only true vodka, Russian vodka. Blindfold me and I'll undertake to spit out whatever Polish, Finnish or Swedish substitutes may be served.

If anything had been needed (which it wasn't) to confirm me in my dislike of the works of Somerset Maugham it was a sordid little passage in one of them extolling Polish zubrovka. Sasha and Igor used to manufacture their own pertzovka by marinating chili peppers in vodka and that was as combustible a brew as ever I met with. On great occasions they would also produce a variety called starka which tasted as though it had just been spewed up from Krakatoa. But zubrovka with its single blade of hay or straw or whatever it is - that's roughly as zesty as clippings from a suburban lawn. Mr Maugham's tribute is now to be seen on the label of zubrovka bottles. Well, I always thought he'd make a good copywriter...

Igor and Sasha both had some sort of official position -

otherwise, in those days, they'd never have been let out of the workers' paradise - but it didn't seem to weigh too heavily on them. They were, after all, Slavs to whom bureaucratic activities came a long way behind vodka in their scale of priorities. As a matter of fact, they were so overwhelmingly Slav that there were times when I wondered if they were any more Russian than Deasey was Irish. They were given to enveloping me and each other and anyone else who happened to be around in prodigious bear hugs. At some stage they inevitably started hurling their glasses at the wall. They moved with bewildering suddenness from clownish high spirits to fierce inconsolable gloom. They were great fun.

They were also a great danger. Dining or lunching with either of them was, to say the least, hazardous. Access to the Soviet Embassy's commissary meant access to unlimited vodka. Caviar, too. Both were served in fearful quantities. A smallish bottle of vodka containing 33 centilitres was given to each of those present by way of an aperitif. When we finally sat down at the table, there was a much larger bottle before each place. You were required, unless you wanted to be vehemently insulted, to empty it in the course of the meal. To merit Sasha's and Igor's respect you were expected to dip into a second bottle. To accompany the coffee at the end of dinner, you could just get away with it if you opted for Armenian brandy (a memorably horrible drink) or champagne from Georgia (where it should have remained). But if you wanted to be regarded as a decent member of society, why! you gulped a few more glasses of vodka. By then, Igor and Sasha were ready to apply themselves to the drinking of vodka.

From time to time, the three of us would dine in a Georgian restaurant, a restaurant that deserves a place in any history of drinks and drinking. It was run by two brothers, in their early sixties I fancied and astonishingly sprightly for their age. Fancy is right. When I got to know them, I ventured to ask one of them how old he was.

"Eighty-eight!"

"Impossible!"

"But true."

"And your brother?"

"He'll be ninety-one next July."

"My God! How do you do it?"

"Vodka. I had my first taste when I was about twelve and I've never drunk less than a bottle a day ever since, neither has my brother. Now I'll tell you something about drinking vodka. First of all, you must empty your glass in one gulp - you know that, of course. No sniffing and sipping like one of these Frenchmen with their wines. Then - and this is the important thing - you must always take a swig of mineral water after every glass. You're a young fellow" (I was about fifty at the time) "and if you do as I say you'll live to be a hundred. Well ninety, at any rate. Because to be sure of reaching a hundred it ought to be Georgian mineral water. For that matter, it ought to be Georgian vodka. And ideally you ought to drink it in Georgia. Those damned Russians..."

"I can get Georgian mineral water at the Embassy", Igor said when the old boy had gone off to attend to another customer. "Next time we come here I'll bring him a case."

He did, too, and presented it with a little speech in Russian which naturally I couldn't understand. The old proprietor made what I took to be a civil expression of his appreciation, also in Russian. Igor looked a trifle disconcerted.

"What did he say?" I asked.

"He said he was glad that there was at least one Russian with enough decency to return something of what the Soviets had pinched from Georgia."

***

Our Georgian restaurant was unique. Its owners, when one went there for the first time, looked one over very carefully. If you were approved of (I never found out what criteria were used for the evaluation) you were made welcome whenever you chose to return. If you failed to pass the test, you hadn't a chance of being admitted then or thereafter. There were times when the Russians and I would be the only remaining customers. Some wretched outcast would turn up, not having yet realised that he was persona non grata. One of the brothers would arrest him at the door.

"Monsieur?"

"I'd like a table for four."

"Impossible - not a single place left."

"What! And all those empty tables?"

"All reserved."

It wasn't enough to be admitted, either. You had to go through a probationary period. For some weeks or months the brothers kept an eye on you. It was very easy to get yourself slung out with no chance of a reprieve. The worst transgression of all was to adulterate your vodka. I've seen one couple expelled merely for asking if they could have a Bloody Mary. God knows what would have happened to anyone who tried to add Coca Cola or some similar syrup to the sacred liquor. The only concession the brothers made was

was in allowing Sasha and Igor to half-fill a beer glass with vodka and then top it up with champagne. I was revolted and told them so. "Ya Russki", they replied in chorus as if that both explained and justified them. "That's right", said the presiding brother with a perceptible sneer, "they're Russians".

If you were one of the elect you could loiter in the Georgians' restaurant for the whole afternoon and most of the night (Igor and Sasha and I often did), you could enjoy frequent rounds of vodka on the house and you could run up bills to virtually any amount. The brothers were civilized men.

"Suppose we never make another centime", one of them explained to me, "we'll have enough to live on. Why on earth should we be bothered by every damned nuisance who pushes in here? Have another glass of vodka."

For all I know, the two old Georgian brothers are still going strong. They'd only be somewhere between 110 and 130. Sasha and Igor, alas, were eventually recalled to Moscow: no doubt their association with Western me had been noted and declared flagitious. I've lifted a glass of vodka to them and their riotous company more than once since they left.   Na zdarovye!

ROUND TEN

From time to time, contentedly tippling, I've reflected that all my shortcomings as a writer can be attributed to the fact that, as I said at the outset, I drink because I like it. I need no traumas to give me a thirst. Real writers drink for definite and invariably painful reasons and get more and more doleful as they do so. Somebody ought to write a doctoral thesis on the subject and, since every other conceivable subject has already been cornered, somebody undoubtedly will.

The earnest aspirant to a PhD will have to bypass a handful of writers, certainly. But the omission of inconvenient facts has always been accepted practice among academics. He - or more probably she - will find very scanty material in Richard Aldington or Roy Campbell who, as I've tried to make clear, were both of them cheerful drinkers. You could even say that they drank because they were cheerful, to celebrate their own abounding enjoyment of life.

A pity there haven't been more like them. Practically all the writers I've met (apart from the madcaps of my Australian youth) and practically all those I've read about drank with grim application and turned morose or pugnacious or plain silly as soon as they'd swallowed a glass or two. Dylan Thomas's performances, of course, have been so exhaustively, not to say exhaustingly, chronicled in every-one's memoirs and sobbingly recalled over every London bar counter that it wouldn't be worth mentioning them if they hadn't been more or less consistently draped in tragic romanticism. Well ... On the rare (I'm happy to say) occasions when I met him he was usually incoherent and always filthy. It was his unvarying custom to make uncouth advances to any women in the vicinity although he would clearly have been incapable of doing anything about it if ever they'd been fool enough to succumb. In between these spasms of crapulous lechery he generally took a wild swing at some nearby male thereby propelling himself into an unsteady rotatory motion and ending up on the floor without anyone having laid a finger on him. Whatever dramas may have been going on behind that pouchy face, there was nothing tragic or romantic perceptible to the onlooker.

I'm not sure, though, that I didn't prefer Thomas's gruesome cavortings to Somerset Maugham's bleak ability to make the drinking of an aperitif resemble a suicide pact. The only time I found myself in the presence I was served (no choice being offered to the lacklustre gathering) with a dry martini. No doubt, this acidulated compound was well suited to Maugham's sour temperament. Personally, I loathe it. After a civil sip, I put my glass down, unobtrusively I thought. Not, apparently, unobtrusively enough. I was young at the time and reasonably prepossessing and I fancied on my arrival that Maugham had looked at me with a trace of concupiscence. It didn't last. The lovelight died. As the friend who had taken me along explained later on, I had committed the supreme offence. You weren't allowed to dislike dry martin is, especially not Somerset Maugham's dry martinis. Maugham, I realised, with his ridiculous laws and directives was just another wowser glimpsed in a looking glass.

Enough of this name-dropping. Besides, now I come to think of it, I haven't got any other names to drop. Perhaps, though, a glance at the biographies of various contemporary writers will furnish a few themes for that Ph.D. thesis on scribbling drunkards. What about Ernest Hemingway now? Expanding his biceps to bursting point, he was constantly letting it be known what a prodigious drinker he was, enumerating the number of glasses or bottles consumed in chronometrically timed periods, carefully identifying the nature of the drinks, sometimes even identifying the brands. The one thing missing - as in the comical divagations of the analysts and sociologists - is any suggestion that all this swigging and swilling gave him the slightest pleasure.

Half of the literary toss-pots, in fact, seem to have overlooked the possibility that drinking might be enjoyable. Quite possibly they actually disliked alcohol. They may even have gone further than those hypothetical Americans at whom the vodka advertisements were aimed and disliked the effects as much as the taste. One gets the feeling that they drank primarily out of respect for some banny ethical system to which they attached themselves. In Hemingway's case, it was the cult of hairiness and sweaty shirts and being one of the boys which required him to belt down all that rum and gin and whisky.

Consider G.K.Chesterton as another example. No sweaty shirts for him but nonetheless in his own way he, too, gives the impression of drinking self-consciously, artificially so to speak. He had his own cult, very different to Hemingway's but still a cult, the cult of an impossible Merry England (should that perhaps be Merrie England?).

> St. George he was for England,
> And before he killed the dragon
> He drank a pint of English ale
> Out of an English flagon ...

Or

Before the Roman came to Rye or out to Severn strode,
The rolling English drunkard made the rolling English road,
A reeling road, a rolling road, that rambles round the shire,
And after him the parson ran, the sexton and the squire;
A merry road, a mazy road, and such as we did tread
The night we went to Binningham by way of Beachy Head.

Rollicking stuff, of course, but when you come right down to it not much more convincing than Hemingway's spurious catalogues of his daily consumption. It's not what a genuine drinker would write out of pure chop-licking enjoyment of a good brew. Let's agree that Chesterton liked an occasional flagon well enough; but you can tell that he emptied it above all as a preliminary to the serious work of propaganda on behalf of that Merry England of his. As a drinker, he belongs to the same school as all those boring Georgians who distanced themselves from "modernism" and "decadence" by playing incompetent cricket and drinking unpalatable beer.

***

It's bad enough when writers like Hemingway and Chesterton exploit alcohol for the purposes of their private cults or play-acting. Worse, as far as I'm concerned, are the melancholiacs, the gloomy drinkers, It's American writers who seem to be the most numerous in this category. If they had to go in for literature, then they should have become linotype operators like H.L.Mencken's beer-swilling friend Bill who thought nothing of downing thirty or forty bottles in a row without shedding a single tear. He didn't, in fact, shed liquid in any form.

Physiologists tell me that these prodigies must have been optical illusions, for there is not room enough in the coils and recesses of man for so much liquid... but Bill avoided the door marked "Gents" as diligently as if he had been a debutante... He would have been humiliated beyond endurance if anyone had ever seen him slink through it.

How much happier they would have been, the Scott Fitzgeralds and the John O'Haras and the rest of them if they'd only switched from writing books to printing them. Compare William Seabrook, forgotten now but a better than best seller in his day, with good old Bill:

I had become a confirmed, habitual drunkard, without any of the stock alibis, or excuses. My health was otherwise excellent; I had plenty of money in the bank, a pleasant home on the French Riviera; my work had been going well enough until the drink put an end to it and promised soon to put an end to me. Then I had tried to stop - and couldn't. I knew that I was killing myself by drinking, and I did not want to die.

Sad; and I'll willingly shed a tear if I must over the spasms of creative sterility, the obtuseness of critics, Oedipus Complexes, writer's cramp or whatever else may afflict America's scribbling alcoholics. Where they forfeit all sympathy - mine, anyway - is in their use of alcohol as an antidepressant. Wine (especially if it's a La Tache), vodka (Russian vodka), rum (from Queensland), absinthe (only a memory) are too noble, too jubilant, too full of the warm South (even if they come from the chilly East) to be employed as a sort of baby's comforter.

ROUND ELEVEN

To exalt, enthrone, establish and defend,
To welcome home mankind's mysterious friend:
Wine, true begetter of all arts that be;
Wine, privilege of the completely free;
Wine, the recorder; wine the sagely strong;
Wine, bright avenger of sly-dealing wrong ...

The frisky benign devil who looks after drunkards led me to settle in the country. He saw to it, of course, that I landed in a wine-growing district - the Sancerre region in the Loire valley. In Australia, say, or America, the estates are dispersed: leaving one you can get a very dry throat before you reach the next. In France, the vineyards chummily adjoin each other, not even separated by a token fence. The Sancerre region comprises about 2000 hectares. There are some 400 full-time growers. They are the only ones who work full time at their profession because everyone else - butcher, baker and candlestick-maker - rightly cuts into his day-to day activities in order to grow a little wine on his own account. The region is a magic circle within which you couldn't get away from wine even if you wanted to and, as that nice devil was well aware, I didn't want to.

***

The righteous minds of innkeepers
Induce them now and then
To crack a bottle with a friend
Or treat unmoneyed men,
But who hath seen the Grocer
Treat housemaids to his teas
Or crack a bottle of fish-sauce
Or stand a man a cheese?

Chesterton, it's clear, didn't frequent the right sort of grocer. My own local grocer never stood me a bottle of fish-sauce - and I wouldn't have thanked him if he had - but more than once and unsolicited he served me a glass of wine of his own making. So, needless to say, did every vigneron with whom I came into contact. They wanted to sell their wine, certainly, but at the same time they took a proper pride in their product. They knew that wine was not only something to be sold but something to be shared. They enjoyed serving you with a glass and watching anxiously to see whether you appreciated it. By the same token, I was only too happy to pay for my weekly intake of bottles; but the convivial sharing of a glass or two raised the transaction to a higher level. It ceased to be purely commercial. An element of humanity was introduced thereby.

***

My pleasure at joining a wine-grower friend or, for that matter, the village grocer or the local carpenter, would every so often be further irradiated as I compared the present conviviality with a trip I'd made to Germany a year or so earlier. The idea was to gather material, as really serious scribblers like to say, for a book which never got written. What was the best starting point? The Moselle region, of course - where else? I spent two days going from cellar to cellar. Thirsty work! Because, whatever pantomime I performed - wiping the sweat from my forehead, coughing drily, reeling back and clutching at my throat, commenting insistently on the warmth of the day - not once was I offered a drop of that golden wine I liked so much. Finally, I asked one grower if I could buy a bottle of his wine. I could. Perhaps he'd like to join me? He would. When we'd emptied the bottle and I'd paid for it he said good-bye.

I was confirmed in my decision not to become a naturalized German when I visited an army headquarters. The duty officer was instructed to show me around. He was very informative. If I'd been listening I would have learnt a lot about half-tracks and self-propelled guns. But it was hideously hot, as hot as Aden, far too hot to concentrate on what he was saying. All I could concentrate on was the prospect of a drink. We came to the officers' mess.

"Here we have the officers' mess."

"And very nice, too."

"Here the officers come to drink their beer."

"So I see. Looks good."

"It is good. Our German beer is very good. It is most thirst-quenching."

"I'll bet it is."

"It enjoys an international reputation."

"And deserves to. This is just the weather for a tankard, wouldn't you say? It's a really blazing day, isn't it?."

"Yes, it is."

There was a pause. It lasted a long time. We watched the flower of the German army drinking its beer. I cracked.

"Perhaps you'll allow me to offer you a glass."

"That would be most pleasant. It is, as you say, a blazing day."

In a British or Australian or French mess, a visitor who suggested buying a drink would be lucky to get off with a horse-whipping. The German army was apparently not so punctilious.

"Your good health." I thought of adding "you son of a bitch" but I didn't.

"Prosit! You pay over there"

I paid.

***

The absence of this Teutonic parsimony was only one of the things in my neck of the Gallic woods for which I was grateful. There was also a blessed absence of the stupefying oenological claptrap which "lovers of wine" indulge in. You didn't hear it in Australia, not in my day at any rate - you probably do now; but in New York and London and even in Paris I'd had to listen, writhing as I did so, to some of the most highly scented flowers of speech since Amanda M. Ros. Evelyn Waugh invents a conversation in *Brideshead Revisited* which is not all that much more fatuous than a dozen such exchanges I've reluctantly overheard myself.

'... It is a little, shy wine like a gazelle.'

'Like a lepprechaun'

'Dappled, in a tapestry meadow.'

'Like a flute by still water.'

'... And this is a wise old wine.'

'A prophet in a cave.'

'... And this is a necklace of pearls on a white neck.'

'Like a swan.'

'Like the last unicorn.'

Listening to similar buffoons I made some discoveries. In my untutored way, for instance, I'd always thought that wine tasted of grapes. Not on your life. This one was redolent of sun-warmed elderberry leaves with the merest touch of nutmeg, that one hinted furtively at a blend of cardamon, cactus and sweet peas, another was dominated by the unmistakable whiff of broccoli.

My vigneron friends - who, after all, knew something about wine - didn't go in for this sort of sacerdotal exegesis. A commendatory grunt if the wine was good, a dismissive thrusting out of the lower lip if it was not what it should be - that was the extent of their commentaries.

***

They drank without undue ceremony, too, and that again was a relief. The Anglo-Saxon wine-bibbers I'd come across sipped with a lugubrious earnestness as if engaged on a critical and perhaps perilous scientific experiment. I got the impression that they would have been more at ease if their wine had been served in test tubes.

***

Wine wasn't the only nourishment provided by the vineyards of the Sancerrois. Once a year, shortly after harvest time, the alambic, the mobile still, would trundle regally from village to village. I've written about this noble thingumajig elsewhere but for the benefit of the scattered few who may not have read my earlier account, it must be celebrated anew.

Mounted on high wheels, dominated by a tall chimney and swathed in inexplicable coils, pipes and taps, the still bore a spooky resemblance to a coupling of Stevenson's "Rocket" with H.G.Wells's time machine. At its feet, the local wine-growers would lay, like propitiatory offerings, all the detritus left over from the grape-pressing. This unappealing refuse was fed into the contraption, the fire was lit beneath the cauldron, a suffocating, a stupefying, an almost visible stink enveloped the countryside and, slowly, drop by drop, from the extremity of one of the pipes emerged a translucent spirit

of incomparable flavour and frightening potency - mare!

Guided by the wise men of the district, I learnt to drink my mare young. It's relatively smooth when it has been aged in the wood for a year or two - only relatively but nevertheless too smooth for those who know what's what. In its youth it is unabashedly tough, a juvenile delinquent, and it goes down your throat with a larrikin rasp. For some reason, grappa and other foreign distillates which should be just as good just aren't as good. Marc provides the true drinker with all the satisfaction that cognac and armagnac procure to more refined palates.

A milk-drinking politician - revered by dairymen throughout the nation - long ago slammed a confiscatory tax on mare making it all but impossible for the wine-growers of France to continue distilling. Only a milk drinker, his wits driven astray by the noxious fluid, could imagine that his edict would eliminate mare from our diet. Frenchmen, and especially French wine-growers, can always be relied on to take effective counter measures to the decrees of their politicians. In every commune, some defiant fellow took up the milk-drinker's challenge. Marc, in the natural course of things, is now produced clandestinely and it's a fact which many have observed that it tastes all the better as a result.

***

Less than ten kilometres from my patch of France is the village of Chavignol. My friend Pascal Thomas makes his wine there. A fair proportion of his output is dispensed in the bistro run by his wife Raymonde. A fair proportion of what goes to the bistro is drunk by me.

I've known some hospitable bistros in my time but none to compare with Raymonde's establishment. Ordinary customers ask for a glass of wine and a glass of wine, excellent wine, is what they get; but if you're lucky enough to be a friend of the family, then a glass turns out to mean a bottle, two bottles, three. Of all the places in which I've drunk- and the number must run into hundreds, possibly thousands - I've never drunk with more enjoyment than in the company of Raymonde and Pascal.

ROUND TWELVE

There's no satisfying some people. I'm one of them. Churlish, I know, but the plain truth is that my gratitude for all the drinks I've drunk is diminished by the thought of all the drinks I haven't drunk. Don't imagine that I was simply too lackadaisical to bother with hunting them down. On the contrary. Like any other collector, I was haunted by the notion that somewhere, just waiting to be discovered, was a unique piece. In my case, what I was after was the ultimate drink, the elixir of life, the Philosopher's Stone, and nobody could have been more assiduous in trying to locate it. As soon as I heard of some previously unknown decoction the old shikari woke in me and I was hot on the trail. I bagged some weird things as a consequence.

I was with Igor and Sacha one day when kvass was mentioned.

"Kvass?"

"Don't bother about it. It's nothing."

"How do I know? You Russians couldn't tell the difference between Romanee Conti and a supersaturated solution of salt. All you ever drink is vodka. I've got to try this kvass of yours. It's probably delicious."

"It's horrible, I tell you. It tastes like nothing on earth and you couldn't get drunk on it if you swallowed a bathtub of the stuff."

"You get me some kvass... "

They were right. In as far as it had any taste, kvass tasted horrible It's alcoholic content was about the same as soda-water. Nevertheless, I'd tried it and was momentarily at peace.

I got worked up in the same way when an Irish friend started extolling potheen. I didn't much care for Irish whiskey and there was no reason why I should like potheen any better but I wasn't ready to neglect whatever possibilities there might be.

"You wait. I know a lad in County Wicklow who distils the finest potheen you've ever put your lips to. I'll bring you back a bottle next time I go home."

He did; and it was revolting.

Sooner or later, whatever could be drunk I drank. At one stage I worked on the theory that revelation was to be found in one of the white alcohols. I'd been conscientiously sampling framboise and quetsche and poire for years past and relished them all but none of them held the key to the Absolute. As I continued spooring,   I came on a distillation of holly (and, incredibly, it tasted of holly), another of sloes, another of blueberries, another of gentian root. Here and there, I thought I got a whiff of eternity (emanating in particular from absinthe) but a few more sips and I realised that I was still earthbound.

***

I had great hopes when I was told about mare a la vipere and both aesthetically and gustatorily (if the word exists) it deserved all the praise that my informant bestowed on it. The recipe is simplicity itself calling for courage rather than art and I'm surprised that no Australian wine-grower has had enough initiative to concoct it. With taipans and tiger snakes at his disposal he ought to be able to produce something much more invigorating than could be hoped for from a mere viper.

Be that as it may, inspired peasants in various regions of France (notably in the Beaujolais district) have been making their own version for centuries past. First select your viper, as Mrs Beeton would say, and introduce it into a bottle which is then filled with mare. In its death agonies (or possibly, mare being as delicious as it is, in a spasm of sheer ecstasy) the creature spits out its venom thereby adding a singular and subtle flavour. The concoction is served with the defunct viper preserved in the alcohol - and a very pretty sight it is, too, although I've known certain namby-pamby individuals briefly contemplate the viper coiled up in its last home and resolutely decline to take a sip. Even when assured that it is a recognised specific against rheumatism (and I myself haven't had a twinge since I took my first swig of it) they have persisted in their foolish shudderings.

Well, no-one who's had the good fortune (and the good sense) to sample mare a la vipere can reasonably feel sorry for himself, I suppose. But reasonably or not, I do. Nothing can console me for the fact that I'm condemned to go down to the grave without ever tasting so many other elusive compounds. Nothing could shake my conviction that the great transmutational potion really did exist and that it was precisely among those potions which were outside my ambit and likely to remain so. What a fool I had been not to stop over on one of the the South Pacific islands and try my luck with kava! My edition of the *Encyclopaedia Britannica,* it's true, didn't think much of it:

The drunkenness produced by kava is of a melancholy, silent and drowsy character. Excessive drinking is said to lead to skin and other diseases ...

What of it? I wouldn't have cared how scrofulous I might become if only kava had proved to be the elixir I was after. Or was illumination lying at the bottom of a gourd of palm toddy? Or in a bowl of fermented mare's milk? I would never know. I'm beginning to think I'll never get to try purl, either. Right from the beginning, when I read about it in *Tom Brown's Schooldays,* I was bewitched by the gem-like assonance of the name and from then on I was resolved to see if it were as good as it sounded.

Here a fresh-looking barmaid serves them each with a glass of early purl as they stand before the fire, coachman and guard exchanging business remarks. The purl warms the cockles of Tom's heart and makes him cough. 'Rare tackle that, sir, of a cold morning,' says the guard, smiling . . .

I had a feeling that I'd regard it as rare tackle myself and one of the first things I did when I reached England was to order a glass of purl in a frowsy London pub.

"We don't have much call for foreign drinks."

"What do you mean, foreign drinks? Haven't you ever read *Tom Brown's Schooldays?*"

"No."

That settled that, and after getting much the same response in several other pubs where I encountered either bewildered or derisive stares, I gave up. The English, poor brutes, seem to have made a point of eliminating all the good things they once possessed. Every vile synthetic syrup is readily available but no purl.

No Bishop, either. My yearning for Bishop (always spelt with a capital B for some reason) was provoked by Dickens's *A Christmas Carol.* I wouldn't myself rate that bit of whimsy among Dickens's finest productions but there was one passage which had me all agog, as they say. That was when the born-again Scrooge informs his clerk that they will discuss the latter's affairs "over a Christmas bowl of smoking Bishop". l toiled from pub to pub begging for Bishop. It didn't necessarily have to be smoking, I told the distrustful bartenders. Any old Bishop would do me.

Every time, this innocent request of mine mysteriously provoked an outburst of fury.

"Whadderyer mean, Bishop? We don't have any bloody bishops here. Whadderyer think this is? A bloody cathedral?"

If it hadn't been for a pseudonymous wag who chose to call himself Willam Juniper I doubt if I' d even have known the composition of Bishop. In an improving work which he published under the title of *The True Drunkard's Delight* Mr Juniper explains that Bishop is composed of a roasted lemon stuck with cloves which is simmered together with mace, cinnamon and allspice in a saucepan full of port, a further bottle of port being added at the last moment or, says Mr Juniper, sherry or madeira or both may be substituted for the port.

The True Drunkard's Delight is an entrancing book and I wish it had never been written. It's bad enough to have gone through life deprived of purl and Bishop without being tormented by the forty-five recipes which William Jupiter lists. Forty-five, with such irresistible names as Tewahdiddle and Rumfustian and Auld Man's Milk, and I've never been able to get at one of them! I've sometimes derived a sort of anguished pleasure from meditating on which of Mr Juniper's luscious compounds I'd choose if I had to pick just one of them. Hungerford Park is tempting in all conscience - apples, nutmeg, ginger-beer (home-made, it goes without saying), half a pint of sherry, two and a quarter pints of ale and a half bottle of champagne; but then there's Rumfustian (eggs, strong beer, white wine and gin). In the end, however, my preference is for Egg Ale. I don't see how anyone could fail to respond to a recipe which begins, "To twelve gallons of ale add the gravy of eight pounds of beef. Then place twelve eggs, the gravy beef, a pound of raisins, six oranges and some spice in a linen bag and leave in the barrel until the ale has ceased formenting. Then add two quarts of sack ... "

***

Incorrigible patriot that I am, I was touched to find Mr Juniper paying tribute to a compatriot, John Harding formerly of the Royal Australian Navy. His testament left straightforward and commendable instructions concerning his funeral in 1930.

Do not let any long-faced undertaker get the last few quid I leave behind. Knock up a box yourselves, and cover it with the Union Jack, hire a truck and follow in a couple of taxis ... Stop on the road at the nearest pub and have a drink, for which I leave the sum of 5. I will be waiting outside. Then carry on ... Then when I am secure in the locker ... I request you to proceed back to the club and drink to the memory of your old shipmate and to our next merry meeting on Fidler's Green ...

Now that our rulers have taken to handing out all kinds of distinctions to all kinds of people, a posthumous Australia Order would be a damn sight more appropriately bestowed on Mr Harding than on most of the nonentities who usually get it.

ROUND THIRTEEN

You expect some changes when you return to a place after an absence of thirty years. I thought I was ready for them. Melbourne as the second largest Greek city in the world? I could cope with that even though I'd known an Australia in which virtually every last soul was of Anglo-Saxon or Celtic origin. Meals that were no longer inexorably a leg of lamb and two vegetables? Well, that was bound to happen eventually. And, of course, feminists and anti-elitists and the politically correct wherever you turned – knowing how these pests proliferate, I'd expected that, too.

One thing, I was dead certain, wouldn't have changed, could never change. The pubs, the beautiful sleazy pubs, the smelly old drinking-hells of my youth would still be there, I knew. You'd still, unless the universe had done a back somersault, ingurgitate a rich culture of infusoria with every gulp of beer. You'd still be chucked out at six o'clock. There would still be some murderous brawls as the company trooped outside. Someone would have spewed over your shoes.

Arthur Symons in one of his sketches of Paris life laments that London pubs should so signally lack the amenities to be found in French cafes. How disgusting, he says, that men should be obliged to drink standing up, "like cattle". That's how it had been with us. We stood at the counter bellowing like an unruly herd as we fought to get our muzzles in the trough. I was prepared to bet that Australian drinkers were still standing up at the counter and still bellowing.

I was wrong all along the line. To begin with, Melbourne no longer, as far as I could see, had any pubs. I trudged with growing despondency in search of the various gin mills which were so fresh - well, not perhaps exactly fresh - in my memory. They weren't there. In their place were unfriendly banks, forbidding office blocks, intimidating government departments, dry as the Nullabor, the whole lot of them.

Here and there - very much here and there - one of the ancient pubs had survived. They looked much the same from the outside, inside they were unrecognisable. Customers were sitting down, as if it were the most natural thing in the world. I couldn't believe it. In the past, chairs and tables were considered positively effeminate. I'm not sure they weren't prohibited by law, like practically everything else in those days.

You could not only sit down inside a pub, you could actually - and this was a truly radical change - sit down outside it. I mean, sit down and drink outside, out of doors, in the fresh air. When I was one and twenty, it would have been inconceivable. Drinking was something to be hidden from sight, like a meeting of the Hellfire Club. When my friend Brad Hammond - a superlative guide in such matters - took me to a pub where you could both drink and eat outside and, as if that weren't enough, do so while sitting down, I knew that the Australian Way of Life as I had known it had vanished for ever.

Plenty of discoveries confirmed this judgement. In the past, for instance, the law was based on the assumption that women were too ethereal ever to experience an honest-to-God thirst. Should any of them be so unfeminine as to want a drink, they were condemned to make do with one of the palm-fringed "lounges" of the big hotels and even there they expected to drink tea or lemonade while listening to a string quartet stridulating excerpts from *The Maid of the Mountains*. Yet here they were before my bewildered eyes as bold as brass in pubs, and swigging beer and gin and whisky like so many sailors on shore leave. No better than they ought to be, I said to myself.

Equally disconcerting were the glasses from which they and everyone else were drinking. The begrimed · semi-communal glasses I'd been accustomed to were no longer visible. In this changed world they positively glittered with cleanliness. You wouldn't have been able to detect a single bacillus on them with an electronic microscope.

Nobody gave the impression of spoiling for a fight. Nobody vomited on the floor. Well, I could wait. it wasn't yet six o'clock. That was when things would get back to normal. That was when the fists would start flying, that was when the boys would put the boot in .... Six o'clock came round. Nothing whatever happened, not so much as a "Come outside, yer bloody drongo, and I'll knock yer fuckin' block off". What's more, everyone went on demurely drinking. It was six o'clock and they went on drinking.

That was what finally finished me off. I'd grown up in a country where one was imbued with the notion that to drink anything stronger than barley water after six o'clock would lead to the immediate collapse of society, to riots and rape, arson, infanticide and forgery as well as to Bright's Disease, bubonic plague and choSeeing all these inoffensive drinkers sipping away at six o'clock, seven o'clock, eight o'clock filled me with uneasiness for the future of Australia.

Before I stumbled out in the night wagging my old grey head over the sad decline in our moral standards, I'd had time to notice the bottles displayed behind the bar. It gave me quite a pang to see that Parfait Amour was no longer available but everything else was. Anything that could be found in a Paris cafe was there - Armagnac, Byrrh, Claquesin, Chartreuse and Calvados - Calvados, the great concentrate of apples that thirty years before had lured me to France!

The man next to me ordered a Pernod. Purist that I am, I winced a bit when he topped it up with Coca Cola but nevertheless there it was, Pernod. I remembered the barmaid at the old Four Courts pub who had somehow acquired or inherited a bottle of Pernod, quite possibly the only one in the whole country. She had affixed a sort of eye-dropper to it and when mixing a Southerly Buster for favoured clients would add two or exceptionally three parsimonious drops. That, in my youth, was the extent of Pernod-drinking in Australia.

**

It had become possible to eat in pubs. Like the provision of tables and chairs, this represented a complete reversal of the policy in force when I'd last been in Australia. Back then, you couldn't get so much as an olive or a potato chip or a peanut, not even for ready money. The slogan was, "Make things tough on the customer". Whether this principle was imposed by the politicians or freely adopted by the publicans themselves I couldn't say. Either way, it was rigidly applied. I may be wrong but my recollection is that you couldn't even nibble on a biscuit you'd brought with you.

This new development briefly encouraged me to hope that I'd come on a pub serving something along the lines of that breakfast in *Tom Brown's Schooldays* - kidneys and bacon and poached eggs. What I actually got tended to be rather more exotic - chop suey, chili concarne, moussaka, the same fare that you had to choke down in London pubs. The fact remained that you were no longer obliged by the licensing laws to go hungry as a penalty for having a drink.

***

Parfait Amour wasn't the only thing that had disappeared. Where was the sump oil that used to be sold to us as wine? What had happened to that "sparkling burgundy" which we thought was so delicious? And those unidentifiable grape-based beverages with disquieting names like "Funnel-Web Red" and "Echidna Table Wine"?

The names on the labels, I noticed as soon as I went browsing in a wine shop, were now noticeably less bizarre; but it was the contents that had me gaping incredulously. Something extraordinary had taken place in the thirty years since I'd been away. Jimmy Watson's best didn't come anywhere near the wines that I could now pick off the shelf almost at random.

Because that was the sheer lip-licking wonder of it: you stood a much better than fifty-fifty chance of getting something drinkable - usually very drinkable - by just grabbing the first bottle within reach. Nobody this side of Bedlam would deny that the greatest wines are French. On the other hand, the poor loons who imagine that all French wines must be good because they're French are heading for a nasty attack of disenchantment and a belly-ache to go with it. I ought to know - and, by heaven, I do know. In Australia, and I'll repeat it under oath, I wasn't once even close to heaving.

It would have been perfect if I could have felt the same degree of enthusiasm for the vineyards that produced such admirable wines. That wasn't possible. To begin with, as I remarked earlier, they were too dispersed: I missed the sensation of being in a community where everybody was dedicated to the making of wine.

Then the cellars were a let-down - as far as I was concerned, that is: a health inspector would have been beaming at the sight of them. They were too hygienic altogether for my taste. If I have to choose between sanitation and cobwebs, I'll take cobwebs every time. Besides, surely it is required by divine law that cellars should be underground, that they should be built of stone and that they should have vaulted ceilings...

All the cellar masters I met were cordial. If there weren't too many other tourists present (but there usually were) they were happy to talk about their wines and to pour a glass or two by way of illustrating what they had to say. But I missed the feeling that I was a welcome guest rather than a customer.

***

That was all I missed. Australia had become a drunkard's delight. The southern hemisphere and the northern were at last leaning on each other' s shoulders, holding each other up, hiccupping in harmony.

ONE FOR THE ROAD

Good luck!
Santé!
Prosit!
Na zdarovye!
Salud!
la manuia!
Slainte mbath!

Printed in Australia
AUHW020831200522
363911AU00005B/18

9 781922 698131